ENI

"Our Bibles are stained with holy blood. The cover of every Bible bears the blood of prophets and martyrs who gave their lives to write, preserve, or translate the Holy Scriptures so that we can read God's Word. When we open the Bible, its pages lead us to the blood of Jesus Christ, his sacrificial death by which believers have forgiveness and emancipation from sin. If such a high price was paid so that we could have this Word, we should cherish the Bible with all our being and study it all our days. But alas, God's Word too often sits neglected as if it were of little worth, while professing Christians fill their minds with the words and images of this world. In *The Word Explored*, Dave Jenkins fields an array of motivations and practical insights for hearing, reading, memorizing, meditating on, and obeying the Word of the living God. This is an excellent resource for pastors who desire to call their churches back to the Word, Christians who seek spiritual renewal for themselves and their families, and non-Christians who want to know why Christians make so much of this Book."

Joel R. Beeke, President, Puritan Reformed Theological Seminary, Grand Rapids, Michigan

"In *The Word Explored*, Dave Jenkins is practical. We need books that help us to practice our faith, to live out God's Word. This is such a book. Yet, don't imagine that this work is simply a "how to" book, it is much more than that. Think church history, biography, biblical and applied theology. This book is all of those things *and more*. Dave takes you on a church history journey, a biblically faithful journey, and an immensely personal journey. Most people have a copy of the Bible. Yet, few people actually read the Bible and few of those who do read the Bible actually seek to understand and apply the Bible. This book pushes back against both neglecting Bible reading and biblical illiteracy. Therefore, the seasoned Christian as well as the new convert will find much help in this book. I urge you to read *The Word Explored* and learn how and why to appreciate your Bible."

Ray Rhodes, Author, *Susie: The Life and Legacy of Susannah Spurgeon: wife of Charles Spurgeon* and *Yours, Till Heaven: The Untold Love Story of Charles and Susie Spurgeon*

"Charles Spurgeon once said, 'Visit many good books, but live in the Bible.' Yet in a world with countless messages vying for our attention, we are too easily swayed with a shallow understanding of Scripture. For that reason, I found *The Word Explored* to be a refreshing, compelling, and heart stirring reminder of how crucial it is to know, live, and walk in the truth of God's Word."

Sarah Walton, Author, *Hope When It Hurts* and *Together Through the Storms*

"God has chosen to reveal himself in a book: the Bible. Circumventing the Bible in order to know the way of salvation through Christ, the will of God for our lives, and the sanctifying work of the Holy Spirit is an exercise in futility. *The Word Explored* is a handy go-to book for practical advice on how the believer can immerse themselves in the Scripture and feast from its bountiful table of rich delights. From reading and study to meditation and memorization, Dave Jenkins has given us a work full of advice and counsel in how to explore the unsearchable wonders of the Word of God as we mature into the image of Christ."

Dustin Benge, Provost and Professor at Union School of Theology, Bridgend, Wales

"Dave Jenkins has distinguished himself in recent years by his founding and leadership of that helpful and increasingly popular biblical site Servants of Grace. However, the work that he has taken on now in writing *The Word Explored* not only harnesses and unleashes his considerable knowledge of biblical theology, but most importantly, meets the remarkable need of the hour. I am gratified and honored to recommend *The Word Explored* by Dave Jenkins without reservation, and with the greatest sense of urgency. For this book seeks a vision not unlike that of the great translator and preacher of the English Bible: William Tyndale. Jenkins has proven to be a soldier in the biblical company of Tyndale, Wycliffe, and others who have given their years to making the Bible available and accessible by many."

Michael A. Milton, Provost, Erksine Seminary

THE WORD EXPLORED

To Sarah,
my beautiful wife and best friend

The Word
Explored

DAVE JENKINS

The Problem of Biblical Illiteracy
& What to Do about It

Exploring the Word

Copyright © 2021 Dave Jenkins

Published by: House to House (an imprint of H&E Publishing)
Peterborough, Ontario, Canada
www.housetohousepress.com

Paperback ISBN: 978-1-989174-86-9
eBook ISBN: 978-1-989174-87-6

Contents

FOREWORD

From the day I first met Dave Jenkins until now, he has been passionate about God's Word and God's grace. When he first explained his vision for this book, it seemed to be just the right book for him to bless the body of Christ with. After reading through it, I am certain that it is.

We live in a time when much of what you read and hear pushes against the grain of God's Word. And yet, for ages it has stood the test of time, critique, science, civil war, and liberal assault. God's Word is like an anvil that never changes as it wears down hammers that pound against it. When we give ourselves to know it, cherish it, and use it, our lives are continuously shaped into instruments used for the glory of God. There is just one glaring problem: *many of us do not hunger for it.*

When you think about having a hunger for God's Word, there are probably at least a few of us who will begin to think, *I just don't have time to go deep into God's Word. I wake up at 5am, exercise, then help with the kids, go to my job, work all day, come back home, help with dinner, help with the kids, finally get to shower, enjoy a brief interlude of silence during a very innocent Netflix binge or Instagram scrolling session, then it's off to bed.* Whatever your life stage, you could probably insert any number of other reasonable, meaningful, or even essential activities into that list. But the most common theme is *I just don't have the time.* If we're honest, I believe most of us would acknowledge that we all have the same 24-hours in a day that others do. It's not that we don't have the time, it's that we don't *make* the time. And we don't make the time because we lack hunger. Hunger will make people do desperate things. Hungry people are pro-active. They take initiative. They will strategize and organize to do whatever it takes to get a meal. What if we had that kind of hunger for God's Word?

When Peter wrote his first epistle, he challenged his readers regarding their "hunger" for God's Word, knowing that it would sustain them in the midst of tumultuous times. Though we are not all being burned by fire or slaughtered in the Roman Coliseum for our faith like many of Peter's original readers, Peter's words still prove magnetic, bringing us back to what fuels and feeds our spiritual vitality—God's Word. 1 Peter 2:2-3 says, "Like newborn infants, long for the pure spiritual milk, that by it you may grow up into salvation if indeed you have tasted that the Lord is good." Like newborn babies crave the milk of their mother in order to live, grow, and be sustained, so also everyone who has been born again ought to have a spiritual hunger for the Word of God to live, grow, and be sustained.

If you've tasted that the Lord is good, and I am guessing you have, then your awe of God should be turning into an appetite for his Word. If you've ever wanted that kind of hunger, you're about to get some big-time help.

Costi W. Hinn
President and Founder
For the Gospel

THE PROBLEM OF BIBLICAL ILLITERACY
& WHAT TO DO ABOUT IT

The whole aim of William Tyndale's life was to get the Bible into people's hands so that they could learn about the good news of justification by faith alone in Christ alone. Tyndale had learned about justification by faith when he happened upon Erasmus' Greek edition of the New Testament. Reading the work of Erasmus in Greek gave Tyndale a burden to put an English version of the New Testament into people's hands, which he completed at the cost of his own life. To translate the New Testament into English, Tyndale traveled all around Europe, and in 1525, landed in the city of Worms, Germany. In 1525 Tyndale's version of the New Testament emerged, and from Worms it was transported and distributed all over Europe. In England, Tyndale's work on the New Testament arrived like a nuclear bomb going off in the countryside. King Henry VII, Cardinal Wolsey, Sir Thomas Moore, and many others were very upset at Tyndale. These men also—ironically—bought up most of the copies of Tyndale's translation (in a desperate attempt to prevent others from obtaining a copy), which further financed his work. Meanwhile, these officials made plans to silence his life and witness.

With the help of many friends, Tyndale managed to evade authorities, improve his translation of the New Testament, and begin his work of translation of the Old Testament. His work of translation is pivotal in the history of the English Bible. Yet, as time went on, it became harder and harder for Tyndale to evade the authorities completely. In 1535 Henry Philipps lured Tyndale away from the safety of his home and, instead of ensuring his safety, he assisted in setting a trap for him. Tyndale was then taken to the Castle of Vivorde, the great state prison of the Low Countries, and was accused of heresy. In 1536, Tyndale was condemned as a heretic and was delivered to the secular authorities for punishment. On the 6th of October 1536 Tyndale was brought to the middle of the town square and given an opportunity to recant, which he refused, and was then bound to the cross and strangled. After being strangled, Tyndale was burned by the executioner, who set the wood ablaze with a lighted torch.

Tyndale gave his life for the sake of people being able to read the Bible in their native tongue. Today we need men and women like Tyndale who faithfully translate the Bible into the language of people. We also need men and women who understand the problem of biblical illiteracy so that it can be directly addressed for the sake of people in our local churches learning to read, interpret, and apply the Scriptures to their lives. To directly combat the disease of biblical illiteracy, we need to understand the extent of the infection, which is why we now turn to discover startling statistics that unveil the magnitude of biblical illiteracy.

Frightening statistics about Biblical illiteracy
Researchers George Gallup and Jim Castelli who have looked into this biblical illiteracy epidemic write, "Americans revere the Bible—but, by and large, they don't read it. And because

they don't read it, they have become a nation of biblical illiterates."[1] At this point, you may think that both Gallup and Castelli have overstated their case, but, as the research illustrates, they haven't. George Barna has dedicated his life to researching trends in the Church. His research showcases eye-opening trends in American Christianity, including:

- Fewer than half of all adults can name the four Gospel accounts.
- Many Christians cannot identify two or three of the disciples.
- Sixty percent of Americans cannot name five of the Ten Commandments.[2]

Several surveys further illuminate the problem of biblical illiteracy, highlighting the breadth of the problem:

- Eighty-two percent of Americans believe that "God helps those who help themselves" is a Bible verse.
- Even among "born again Christians," eighty-one percent believe that the Bible teaches the primary purpose in life is to take care of one's family.
- Twelve percent of adults believe that Joan of Arc was Noah's wife.

---

[1] George Gallup and Jim Castelli, *The People's Religion: American Faith in the 90's* (Macmillan, 1989), 60.
[2] *The State of the Bible Six Trends for 2014*, 8 April, 2014, (accessed July 5, 2019. http://www.barna.com/research/the-state-of-the-bible-6-trends-for 2014/#.VkZeQr 9xJpu).

- Over fifty percent of graduating high school seniors thought that Sodom and Gomorrah were husband and wife.[3]

Many Christians rightly believe that they need to read the Bible but do not properly understand how to approach the Word or what its purpose is in their life. In a recent LifeWay Research study, we learn the following about our Bible reading habits among church attendees:

- 19% - Everyday
- 26% - A few times a week
- 14% - Once a week
- 22% - At least once a month
- 18% - Rarely or never.[4]

Almost sixty percent of churchgoers open their Bibles at home during the week at least once. And for every person who reads his/her Bible everyday (nineteen percent), someone else (eighteen percent) isn't reading theirs...at all. Understanding how to hear the Word of God, read the Word of God, and study the Word of God is *vital*. These statistics illustrate the disconnect between proclaiming a Christian identity and understanding Scripture and the biblical worldview. Next, let's consider three aspects of the Holy Spirit's ministry as it relates to the Christian life, and how this ties into reading the Word.

---

[3] *The State of the Bible Six Trends for 2014.*
[4] Biblical Illiteracy by the Numbers.

Three aspects of the Holy Spirit's ministry

The Holy Spirit aims to guide Christians into all the truth in the Word of God, and to point us from the Scriptures to Christ alone for a life of faith, adoration, and service. In John 16:14 Jesus says, "He will glorify me, for he will take what is mine and declare it to you." To understand what Jesus says, we need to consider how the ministry of the Holy Spirit is at work in the world to bring people to Jesus and to empower the people of God to be on mission in making disciples of Jesus.

The Holy Spirit's ministry is to testify to biblical truth (John 14:16–17; 16:14–15). Recently I was talking with a twenty-five-year-old young man in the town where I live who told me in our conversation, "I'm lost." As we continued talking, it became clear that he is searching for meaning, value, identity, and worth in drugs, the pursuit of pleasure, and other things of the world. I then proceeded to walk him through how God desires to sovereignly replace his heart of stone with a new heart, a new identity, and a new purpose in the gospel.

As we consider the subject of the Holy Spirit and biblical illiteracy, what we need to understand is that the Holy Spirit aims to open people's eyes to the truth about Jesus, as he did with the disciples on the road to Emmaus in Luke 24:31. It's not only the young man I mentioned above who is lost, but there are also others, those around you and me, people who we interact with each day, who too are "lost." For example, a husband or wife may abandon their spouse with no biblical support. Someone else might pursue a life of greed and pride or teach unbiblical doctrines or advocate to others in our local churches that they should worship in *any way they see fit*, apart from biblical teaching. Such Christians may claim the leading of the Holy Spirit, but they deceive themselves when they profess Christ but refuse to obey the clear teaching of Scripture. The Holy Spirit aims to serve and glorify Christ alone. To that end, the Holy Spirit doesn't lead people to worship or live how they want, but only according to the revealed Word of God. The ministry of the Holy Spirit is intertwined with the Word of God. As such, to address the problem of biblical illiteracy we need to understand the ministry of the Holy Spirit who is at work in creation, salvation, the local church, and the witness of the people of God.

The ministry of the Holy Spirit
The Holy Spirit is active and at work in the world. Some examples of this include his involvement in creation (Genesis 1:2), in the Incarnation (Matthew 1:18), and in the apostles and prophets as they committed to writing the Bible (2 Peter 1:19–21). The Holy Spirit is sovereignly at work in bringing people to salvation (John 3:3, 5, 8). All Christians possess the indwelling presence of the Holy Spirit at the moment of salvation (Romans 8:9). Christians permanently possess the Holy Spirit (Ephesians 1:13–14). The Holy Spirit's sealing work cannot be undone because it is all to "the praise of his glory" (Ephesians 1:14). Every Christian is to be filled with and led by the Holy Spirit (Ephesians 5:18). The fruits of the Holy Spirit (Galatians 5:22–23) are fruits produced in Christians because of his work in them. Jesus promised the Holy Spirit would be a guide, teacher, and comforter for Christians (John 14:16–18) and he promised that the Holy Spirit would fuel the mission of God through the local church (Acts 1:8).

Through the work of witnessing, which will be carried on by the apostles and their followers (John 15:27), the Holy Spirit will not only lay bare the world's sin, but in the case of some, will awaken a consciousness of guilt which leads to true repentance (1 John 3:8). When the Holy Spirit, through the preaching of the gospel, convicts men and women of their sin, a considerable number of them will cry out, "Brethren, what shall we do?" (Acts 2:37) and turn to Christ in faith and repentance. The Holy Spirit aims to teach Christians about the truth of Jesus so as to drill the truth they have received in the revealed Word of God deeper into their hearts and minds.

The Holy Spirit & reading the Word
The Holy Spirit intends to work in the life of his people, drawing us near to the Lord Jesus, and does so through our reading and studying of the Word.

Earlier I mentioned a twenty-five-year-old man I met in my town. I've met other young men like him. They think they are spiritual, seeking a higher power. Most often they believe in eastern mysticism and believe that new age philosophy is the path to "enlightenment" and the "good life." To these young men (and women) this is the goal of what it means to be "spiritual" and a "good person." And these young people are not alone; I've met many seasoned Christian men and women who believe the same things.

As Christians, when we are speaking of the results of the Holy Spirit's work in our lives, it must always lead us to thankfulness and gratitude for all the Lord has done. See, the result of the Holy Spirit's work in the life of the Christian must always be a keener interest and delight in Jesus' work in our lives, a more fervent love and devotion for Jesus, a firmer trust and reliance on Jesus, and an increased obedience to Jesus.

7

In John 16:7 Jesus says, "It is to your advantage that I go away." Jesus says this because, once he is enthroned in Heaven, he would send the Holy Spirit. It is because the Holy Spirit is working with power in our hearts that we (the people of God) are drawn into closer discipleship with the Master than was even possible for the original disciples. By the Holy Spirit, true believers possess a more blessed experience—through union with Christ—of the saving benefits that he has provided for his people, so they may commune with him in their daily lives.

Solving biblical illiteracy

Among many others throughout the history of the church, William Tyndale aimed the course of his life towards one end: the glory of God. A ship has an aim. It does not leave the harbor for just *any* reason. For example, a fisherman doesn't just set out to go on an expedition. He has a purpose in mind and knows what he wants to catch. The aim of the Christian life is the same. The Christian moors in the safe harbor of Christ alone, in whom he invites his people to find rest, strength, and hope; he is their rock of refuge (Psalm 18:2), a present help in time of need (Psalm 46:1), and a comforter for those experiencing affliction (Psalm 119:50; 2 Corinthians 1:4; 1 Thessalonians 3:7).

See, the problem of biblical illiteracy is one we cannot ignore anymore; it is one that local churches must address. All around us are people like the young man I mentioned previously who strive to find meaning, value, identity, and worth in the things of this world, only to wind up proclaiming "I'm lost." The infection of biblical illiteracy spreads within the church as well. Seasoned men and women sit in our pews, year in and year out, listening to the sermons of pastors and Bible study teachers who don't know how to read, study, and apply the Bible. This is a problem that is not going away, and it's one that we must remedy with Scripture. To do that, Christians need to understand the connection between the Word of God and the Holy Spirit. Jesus calls his Church to a rescue mission of declaring to the lost that Christ alone can find and redeem the lost (Luke 19:10). Additionally, he uses Christian men and women for his glory by equipping them in the local church through the preaching and study of the Word of God (Ephesians 4:14–15).

If the Church fails in this urgent task, people in our churches will not understand that they've been sent by the Holy Spirit into the world as witnesses for the glory of Christ alone. Additionally, they will not understand how the Holy Spirit illuminates the Word for the sake of growth in the love of Christ. They also won't understand how the Holy Spirit continues to convict, comfort, and encourage the people of God through the personal and corporate reading of the Word.

Now that we've outlined the problem of biblical illiteracy, we must continue marching on to understand, not only the problem, but what to do about it, by turning now to the topic of hearing and reading the Word.

1

HEARING & READING THE WORD

Hearing the Word

It could be argued that the easiest of the spiritual disciplines is to hear the Word of God. Healthy Christians develop the regular practice of attending a local church where God's Word is faithfully preached. Consider the words of Paul in Romans 10:17: "So faith comes from hearing, and hearing through the word of Christ." While this verse is teaching about initial faith, we need this kind of faith day-to-day. For example, hearing about God's provision may aid a family to trust God through their difficult financial situation. Perhaps hearing a biblically based sermon on the love of Christ may be God's means of granting assurance to a downcast believer. Afterall, "man does not live on bread alone but on every word that comes from the mouth of the LORD."[1]

All around us are messages that are inundating our hearts and minds, vying for our affections, and confronting our worldviews. The question is not *whether* we are being impacted by these messages, but whether we are hearing those messages and then *believing* them. Jesus tells us repeatedly that what bubbles up from our lives begins in our hearts and moves outward from there.[2] What we input into our lives, what daily bread we feast on, will make its way into our hearts. This is why we must be careful what we hear (or read).

When we hear or read a message, we must be like the Bereans in Acts 17:11. Paul commends the Bereans because they searched

---

[1] Deuteronomy 8:3.
[2] Luke 6:45.

11

the Scriptures to see if "these things are so." True discernment uses the mind, and all the faculties and resources the Lord has given us, so that we can obey him. If faith comes from hearing, then we must be sure we feast on Scripture-based truth.

Samuel hearing the voice of the Lord
Samuel is the last of a long line of judges in Israel and the first— in the genuine sense of the word—prophet in the Old Testament. That being said, Samuel didn't know the voice of God because he didn't know God. 1 Samuel 3:4–8 tells us that Samuel went to Eli, the high priest at the time. As a young lad, Samuel woke up in the middle of the night and went three times to Eli, asking about the voice he'd heard. Finally Eli caught on to what Samuel was hearing. Samuel was hearing from none other than the *Lord*! What Samuel needed was help to hear from the Lord. He needed to hear the instructions the Lord had for him regarding his life. Finally, picking up on these things, Eli tells Samuel to go and lay back down and tell the Lord "Speak, LORD, for your servant hears."[3]

Today, we too must learn to discern the voice of the Lord, but unlike in Samuel's day, we have the sixty-six books of the Bible that constitute the authoritative Word of God. We do not need additional revelation from God. In order to hear from God, all we must do is crack open that Bible and read the Word of God *directly*. It's critical to understand that when the Scriptures speak, God speaks. So, if you want to hear from the Lord God, you do not need a higher power, another teacher, a guru, or anything of the like. If you want to hear from God, you don't need *another* mediator, you need the Mediator Jesus Christ, who is revealed in the Scriptures. To hear from God, you first

---

[3] 1 Samuel 3:9.

must be *born again*. Only then can you hear what God has to say through his Word, as he opens your eyes to the truth of Scripture and points you to Christ alone.

Hearing from the Lord is not only an individual concern. The New Testament epistles begin by addressing the local *church*. When the epistles were received by the local church, they were then read outloud to the people. Likewise, we not only hear God speak from the Word in our own personal reading time, but we also hear God speak through our pastor in our local church.

A real love for God is evidenced by a love for what God loves.[4] Paul tells Christian men in Ephesians 5:25, for example, they are to love their spouse because "Christ loved the church and gave himself up for her." Obedience to God and cultivating a love for what he loves isn't an individual operation in the Christian life. We need Christ and we need one another which is why we need the local church.

In our local churches we need each other as we sit under the faithful expository ministry of our pastor who preaches the Word of God. In chapter six we will consider more in depth our pastor's responsibility to preach the Word of God and church members' responsibility to hear, heed, and obey the Word of God.

Hearing the Word of God and exercising discernment
True Christians are to have a genuine desire to hear from God through his Word. Christians long to hear from God, both privately and corporately, because of Christ who has placed within them new desires—through the new birth—to hunger

---

[4] John 15:8–11; Ephesians 5:25.

and thirst for the final revelation of God found in the Scriptures, which testify of the redemption Christ has won for them. To cultivate a genuine and earnest longing for more of the Lord, we need to hear from God in his Word. This is how we are to grow in grace. We need the Word of God. If we say we love the Lord and don't have any genuine desire, or never have a longing to hear from God in his Word, then how can we say love the Lord? True Christians love what God loves—and God loves his Word and the local church.[5]

I'm not aiming to point a finger in your face and reveal the defects in your Christian life; although I am praying the Lord will bring conviction to you through the Holy Spirit. Further so, my aim is not to guilt you into going to church to hear the Word, but rather it is to get you to see that you, as a Christian, are surrounded by messages that run contrary to the Word of God. This is why you need to not only hear from God on the Lord's Day through the preaching of God's Word, but also why you need others in your local church who can help you grow in the grace of God.

What we listen to reflects what we love
In Luke 11:28 Jesus says, "Blessed rather are those who hear the word of God and keep it!" So merely listening to God-inspired words is not the point. Hearing the Word should lead to *obedience* to God's commands, which yields Christ-likeness.

What we hear and digest into action will become a reflection of what we love. My wife and I regularly tell each other, "I love you." We do that because we mean it. But it's not enough for me to *say* that I love my wife. If I don't listen to her when she is speaking into my life, I am not loving her. I am not showing her that she

---

[5] Ephesians 5; 2 Timothy 3:16.

14

is important, valuable, and precious to me. Similarly, if my wife is sharing openly and honestly about her day and her struggles, frustrations, challenges, and good things that happened to her that day, and I just tune her out or refuse to listen to her, I am not loving her. Yet, many Christians do this to God—the same God who has saved us, is sanctifying us, and who will one day glorify us. Instead of genuinely hearing God, who speaks today through the preached Word of God and our reading of the Word, we would rather tune him out and tune into sports, or a television psychologist, or a self-help guru.

Perhaps you feel guilty about how you spend so much time watching television or movies. There are some who say it's a complete waste of time to watch television, so let me say that I *do* watch television. I watch television shows and sports (especially Golf Channel and anything NFL related). I am not saying that you shouldn't watch television or any such thing—that is a decision between you and God—but I am saying this: those you listen to and whose message you take to heart will shape you. In Proverbs 4:23 we are taught to guard our heart with all due diligence because everything we do flows from the heart. What Jesus promises to believers in John 7:38 is nothing less than streams of living waters flowing from our hearts through the new birth, because the Holy Spirit resides in his people.

We prioritize what we love
I love my wife. I want to hear what she has to say, so I prioritize her accordingly. When she speaks, I want to listen because I love her. How much more should we who are Christians do the same with God? How much more should we long to hear the preached Word of God and to read it? We, who have been born again, should long for the perfect Word because it tells of the

great and grand story of redemption—that Christ has won the day and is soon returning. Everywhere throughout redemptive history, Christ is ruling and reigning, orchestrating good for us in evil and challenging times. He is conforming us into the image of God through the daily challenges of our lives. In order to grow in his grace and have the strength to face daily challenges, we must hear the voice of God and be pointed back to the firm foundation in his Word.

He longs for his people to hear from him, to heed what he has said, and obey his voice. Yet, James 1:26 is right in that many of us would rather be *hearers* only and not *doers* of the Word. We say with our lips that we love the Lord, and yet with our lives we often spurn him, acting as if the costly sacrifice of Christ doesn't matter at all. Because I love my wife, I prioritize her. Likewise, if we love Christ, we will prioritize him in our lives; not just by hearing the Word preached on Sundays, though that is vital, but daily through personal Bible reading.

Personal Bible reading
One of the most significant needs for a Christian is to open his or her Bible and read it. You may have decided that this was going to be the year when you read through the entire Bible. You may even have been regularly reading your Bible and be at the point where you've reached Leviticus (or one of the other books of history) but have stopped. I understand how that is, and have been there before. When this happens, we need to understand that—for example, in the case of Leviticus—while it's full of many laws, the point of this book is to reveal the holiness of God.

As Christians, we've been given a Book (the Bible) that is *not* a fairytale or myth. The Word of God is *living water* to the

Redeemed,[6] Bread of Life to the hungry,[7] and a treasure to all who call on the name of the Lord God.[8] Through the Word, Christians can delight in the Lord who delights in them now, in and through Christ.[9]

One of the reasons why we're often so depleted in the Christian walk is because we don't spend *substantive, meditative, and reflective* time in the Word of God. At the heart of substantive time in the Word is being intentional about reading our Bible, even if it's only for 5-10 minutes. We want to see this time as an opportunity to slow down and cherish what we are reading. Further, we ought to meditate on what we read, reflecting on how it shapes our lives. We don't read the Bible as a book full of information and facts. We read the Bible because it is the means of God to help his people grow in his grace. We will return to the topic of substantive, meditative time in the Word in chapters three and four.

Daily Bible reading: delight or duty?

Whenever I write or speak about the need for Christians to daily read their Bibles, I almost always get some form of pushback. At the heart of most of the pushback I hear is something along the lines of how I am "making Bible reading a duty, rather than a delight." 2 Timothy 3:16-17 reads, "All Scripture is breathed out by God and profitable for teaching, for reproof, for correction, and for training in righteousness, that the man of God may be complete, equipped for every good work." Here, Paul helpfully guides readers to understand the power of reading the Bible: equipping us, the servants of God, for the

---

[6] John 7:37-38.
[7] John 6:5.
[8] Hebrew 11:26; 1 Timothy 6:18-19; Luke 12:34.
[9] Psalm 1:2; Psalm 37:4; Psalm 119:35.

work laid out for them. As Christians living in biblically illit-
erate times, as we considered in the introduction to this book,
we need to honestly ask ourselves how we are going to stand
for what the Bible says if we don't daily read or listen to Scripture; if we don't *know* what those Scriptures say.

Furthermore, in 1 Timothy 4:7–8, Paul exhorts Timothy
to discipline himself in godliness: "Have nothing to do with ir-
reverent, silly myths. Rather train yourself for godliness; for
while bodily training is of some value, godliness is of value in
every way, as it holds promise for the present life and also for
the life to come." In this way, reading the Bible isn't merely a
duty, but a duty accompanied with a promise, both presently
and to come.

At this point, some people may think that this chapter is
just a ploy to guilt them into reading their Bible daily. This
couldn't be further from the truth. While being in the Word
daily is a duty, it is also a delight.

A delightful duty
Daily Bible reading is a *joy*. When daily Bible reading is something we check off of our spiritual checklist, then we will never
grow in righteousness, nor will we ever discipline ourselves for
godliness. I love my wife, and so delight in time spent with her,
getting to know her better. Matthew 22:37–38 calls us to
"'love the Lord your God with all your heart and with all your
soul and with all your mind.' This is the great and first commandment." By coming under his Word, *daily*, we not only
begin to know the Lord better, but we begin to delight in him
more.

Matthew 22 goes on to say in verses 39 and 40, "And a
second is like it: You shall love your neighbor as yourself. On

these two commandments depend all the Law and the Prophets." It is impossible to love God or others without God. We read, study, and meditate on the Word so that the Holy Spirit may convict and apply the Word to our lives, with the result of God's people growing in his grace.

A Christian's growth in grace is not an option, it's a command.[10] Daily Bible reading is where we discipline ourselves, allowing his Word to soak into our souls. The Holy Spirit uses the Word in the life of the Christian to help him or her delight more in Jesus than in him or herself. The Bible is the ultimate love letter, given by God to help his people know and serve him by revealing the inexhaustible depth of his love.

So please, pick up your Bible and allow yourself to grow in the grace and knowledge of our Lord and Savior, Jesus Christ. As you do, you'll find yourself not only growing in your understanding of God's Word, but also in that your heart and mind are daily thinking on what is *noble, pure, good, holy, and just.* There's nothing better for God's people to do than to joyfully delight in him, through the daily discipline of Bible reading.

Reading the Bible with the church
Reading the Bible, meditating on God's Word, journaling, and reading helpful books about theology are all *crucial*, but solitary. "Until I come," says the Apostle Paul—knowing that his death is imminent, and seizing, perhaps, the opportunity to give direction to the Church for the centuries ahead—further encourages Christians to "give attention" (NASB), or "devote yourself" (NIV), "to the public reading of Scripture, to

---

[10] 2 Peter 1:3–15; 3:18.

exhortation and teaching."[11] It's clear enough what the Apostle Paul wants done in the public assembly of the Church: He wants Scripture to be read.

Terry Johnson rightly explains, "The practice of the synagogue was to unroll the scrolls of Scripture, read a portion, mark where they stopped, and then pick up again the next Sabbath where they left off."[12] And while there is a place for your personal, passionate pursuit of God, the Bible was never meant to remain a solely singular study endeavor. The Word of God has always been a community treasure. These books, letters, stories, poems, laws, and prophecies are meant to be read aloud. It is the call upon the people of God to worship him, through his Word, recounted and recited in the midst of biblical community.

Practical guidance on reading the Word
This chapter has explored why you *should* engage in reading the Bible daily, but perhaps you feel stuck and don't know where to begin. I like to recommend that people start at the beginning of the Bible, in Genesis, and work their way through to the end of Revelation. As you work your way through the entire Bible, you'll get a full picture of God's character and his redemptive plan for the world.

In Genesis, you'll find fascinating stories that help you understand what God is up to in the rest of the Bible such as Abraham, Isaac, Jacob, and Joseph. In Leviticus, you'll discover the laws of God and learn about his holiness. In Exodus, you'll discover the Lord at work in delivering the people of Israel, which

---

[11] 1 Timothy 4:13.
[12] Terry Johnson, "The Public Reading." Ligonier Ministries. July 1, 2009 (https://www.ligonier.org/learn/articles/public-reading/ Accessed June 26, 2020).

provides a beautiful picture of our redemption in Christ. The books of history tell the story of God at work in the life of the people of Israel and their failure and success in keeping the law of God. In the Prophets, you'll discover God reminding the people of Israel who they are and the prophets issuing covenantal warnings and encouragement to return wholly to the Lord. In the books of wisdom such as the Psalms, you'll find brutal honesty from the writers about what's going on in their lives and also more about the character of God.

Perhaps starting at the beginning seems tedious and you still find yourself stuck in your reading. While I encouraged you to start at the beginning of your Bible, flipping over to the New Testament and starting with the Gospel of John is a great way to begin your journey of being in the Word. John's Gospel helps us understand the person and work of Jesus Christ. Another great New Testament book that is a great place to start for those struggling to spend time in the Bible is the book of Hebrews. There you will read about the New Covenant and the utter sufficiency of Christ in and over all things.

If you find yourself feeling discouraged and life is caving in on you, one reason among many is that, as a Christian, if you aren't reading the Word, you are suffocating for lack of spiritual food and water. Reading the Bible is a *need*, just like air and water. Begin to see the Bible not as a collection of information and facts to inform your mind, but as the living Word of God written to humanity from God himself to inflame your heart with a passion for knowing the Lord. Whether you start in Genesis or John, with an hour out of your day or with 10 minutes, I encourage you to be in the Word daily.

Conclusion

Hearing and reading the Word of God is essential for the Christian life. Not only are Christians to hear the Word of God, but they are to read the Word of God, daily. As we continue to read the Word of God every day, we hear the voice of God in all of Scripture. We read the Scriptures to hear the voice of God through the biblical text. Now that we have considered the topic of hearing and reading the Word, we move on in our next chapter to learn how to study the Word of God.

2

STUDYING THE WORD OF GOD

In my early teens, I fell in love with the Bible and with theology. Although I grew up in the church, my appetite to know God more deeply grew rapidly. But while I developed an insatiable appetite for the Word, during my high school years I realized that the point of reading the Bible wasn't to simply fill my head with facts. I could give people the right answers to complex theological questions, but my doctrinal convictions didn't always inform my practice. There was a disconnect between the theology I knew and the life I lived.

In 1 Timothy 4:16 Paul tells Timothy, his young disciple, to watch his life *and* his doctrine. What I missed in my Bible reading was the importance of the Word for Christian living. It is this connection that I hope to convey in this chapter. My hope for you is that you'll not only have sound biblical convictions about the Bible, but that these convictions will form and fuel a passion for right living, right worship, and right study of the Bible—not just for information's sake, but for the sake of loving God and loving others.

Sound doctrine & sound living
Christians are not to avoid doctrine. If we are to steady ourselves in Christ to withstand the storm of cultural upheaval, our convictions must be shaped and molded in the firm soil of the Word. As James 1:22 says, it's not enough to be hearers of the Word only, but we must also be doers of the Word. When the Word of God takes root in his people, it leads to obedience.

This is why Paul reminds Timothy to watch both his doctrine and his life, because the way he lives reveals what he believes.

Christians, when they are born again, are enlivened to believe right doctrine, adore sound doctrine, and love the God who gives us good nourishing teaching. The result of seeing not only the truth but the goodness of sound doctrine leads not only to sound living, mission, and ministry for the glory of Christ, but right worship of him. The Christian faith is one unified picture under the Lordship of Jesus Christ. There is no division in the Lord Jesus, and neither should there be division in the heart, mind, and soul of the Christian.

Why we miss Christ in the Bible
Since all Scripture points to Christ, any appeal to reading or studying the Word should lead readers to Jesus, for it is through the Word of God that he exerts saving power.[1] In John 5:39, Jesus says that the message of all of the Scriptures concern him. Two examples of this include the prophecies of Christ and the meaning of types.

When Jesus said, "It is finished"[2] he brought about the completion of all of the Old Testament prophecies, symbols, and foreshadowing about himself. From the beginning of Genesis to the end of Malachi, there are 300 detailed prophecies about the Anointed One, which are fulfilled by Jesus. From the "seed" who would crush the serpent's head[3] to the "Suffering Servant"[4] to John the Baptist, the messenger of the Lord, who prepared the way for Jesus,[5] all of the prophecies were fulfilled

---

[1] Romans 10:17.
[2] John 19:30.
[3] Genesis 3:15.
[4] Isaiah 53.
[5] Malachi 3:1.

and finished in the life, ministry, and death of the Lord Jesus Christ.

"Types" are persons, events, and institutions that typify something about Jesus Christ: they characterize the coming Messiah and his work. Moses was a type of Christ as our deliverer from bondage. King David was a type of Christ as a faithful king. Solomon typified Jesus' reign of peace and glory. The conquest of Jericho was a type of Christ's conquest over Satan. The tabernacle typified God as he dwells among men through Christ. These stories, or types, help Christians better understand and appreciate the person and work of the Lord Jesus, because unlike the types gone before him, Jesus fulfills these things perfectly and completely.

Since Christ is everywhere in the Bible, even in the Old Testament, time and time again, the most devoted atheists, Buddhists, Mormons, Jehovah Witnesses, etc. have been brought to faith in the Lord Jesus through the Scriptures. One powerful example of this is D.E.V. Rieu, one of the world's great classical scholars, and a lifelong agnostic, who was asked to provide a translation of the Gospels.

When Rieu's son heard that his father was commissioned to translate the Gospels, he commented, "It is going to be interesting to see what Father will make of the four Gospels. It will be even more interesting to see what the four Gospels make of Father." He must have been on to something because, while translating the Gospels, Rieu came to faith and became a committed Christian.[6]

At this point you might ask, "Why doesn't this happen to everyone who reads the Bible?" Throughout Scripture, we see

---

[6] This account is found in greater detail in J.B. Philips, *The Ring of Truth* (Wheaton: Harold Shaw, 1977).

25

the Scribes and the Pharisees searching the Scriptures but failing to see the clear allusion to Jesus and thus failing to put their faith in Jesus. Through their example, we can see that Bible reading alone doesn't lead us to salvation. Rather, Bible reading is a means of grace to point us to the person and work of Jesus, who is the one who does the saving.

This is why it matters not only *how* we approach the Scriptures but *why* we approach the Scriptures. Jesus explains why the Scribes and Pharisees missed the point of Scripture in John 5:39, by starting with their attitude towards the Word. The Pharisees exalted such knowledge, not as a means to grow in knowledge and understanding of God, but as an end to pursue in and of itself. This is why Jesus says in John 5:39, "You search the Scriptures because you think that in them you have eternal life." The Pharisees were not interested in the *message* of Scripture; they were more interested in possessing knowledge than in studying to *know God*.

In my own life, I've had times where I've made a big show of how much knowledge of the Bible I've had. In the end, what I've found in reflecting on these times is that I was not fully living in Christ, but instead running dry and empty. As a result, what I was thirsting for was more of God. Thankfully, God provides drink and food in the Word of God, which I'm to delight in and be satisfied by.

Donald Grey Barnhouse, a well-regarded Bible teacher from the previous century, provides a helpful illustration about the right attitude toward the Bible when he imagines a person standing below a window high in a skyscraper overlooking the ocean. He remarks, "What would we say if the person talked only about the window itself—its dimensions, the kind of material in it, and its construction? We would marvel that he made no mention of the ocean view! Likewise, we must not study the Scriptures as if the Bible itself were our focus."[7] Just as the purpose of a window is to see what's outside, so the purpose of the Bible is to see, know, trust, and love the person and work of Jesus as he is revealed in the Scriptures, so we may be saved by Christ alone, and equipped to serve the Lord Jesus.

The Scribes and Pharisees missed Christ in Scripture not only because their attitude was bad, but also because they had worldly interests and motivations as opposed to heavenly ones. The religious leaders were interested in national pride and victory over the Romans, and didn't adore Christ because he didn't follow these expectations.[8] Rather than loving God and loving others,[9] the religious leaders sought to receive glory from men.[10]

Jesus' ministry was not like the Pharisees'. Jesus was not interested in a popularity contest. In fact, in his mission to save the lost and make disciples,[11] Jesus said hard things, refusing to compromise the Word. When many people deserted him because of these hard teachings, he asked his disciples, "Do you want to go away as well?"[12] Jesus told his followers that he doesn't receive glory from people, and to follow him is to expect scorn from the people of this world.[13]

---

[7] Donald Grey Barnhouse, *Illustrating the Gospel of John* (Grand Rapids: Revel, 1973), 77-78.
[8] John 5:43.
[9] John 5:42; 1 Timothy 1:5; John 5:1-16.
[10] John 5:44.
[11] Luke 19:10; Matthew 28:16-20.
[12] John 6:67.
[13] John 5:41; Matthew 16:24-26.

Studying & searching the Scriptures for profit

John Newton, pastor and the author of the hymn "Amazing Grace," helpfully instructs us that, as Christians, we are to be like miners "who seek their treasures by digging and examining the Scriptures."[14] You and I, as Christians, must study the Scriptures for the aim and purpose of which they were given; that is, to know Christ, and by coming to him, receive eternal life.[15]

When studying the Bible, Christians should pair their time of study with prayer. Psalm 119:18 says, "Open my eyes, that I may behold wondrous things out of your law." Through rebirth by the Holy Spirit, and the gift of prayer, Christians grow in their desire to commune with the living God through reading and studying Scripture.

Imagine a young woman who received a love letter from her fiancée. She would devour such a letter and re-read it time and time again because those words are precious to her. She would read between the lines to see if there were any hidden meaning. In Scripture, we have something even more significant: a love letter from God himself. A.W. Tozer once said, "The Bible is not an end in itself, but a means to bring men to an intimate and satisfying knowledge of God, that they may enter into him, that they may delight in his presence, may taste and know the inner sweetness of the very God Himself in the core and center of their hearts."[16] As you increasingly see God's Word as a love letter, you will delight in searching and studying the precious words of Scripture.

---

[14] *The Works of John Newton*, 6 vols. (1820; repr. Edinburg: Banner of Truth, 1985), 2:322–323.

[15] John 17:3; John 5:39–40.

[16] A.W. Tozer, *The Pursuit of God* (Harrisburg: Christian Publications, 1948), 10.

Growing in passion for the Word

In 1 Samuel 27 through 1 Samuel 29, the narrator of 1 Samuel tells us that King David flees Philistia, where he becomes the bodyguard of Achish, one of the Kings of the Philistines.[17] Throughout 1 Samuel 27–29, David does not consult with the high priest who has the ephod to divine the will of God, but instead is self-reliant. David returns to Ziklag in 1 Samuel 30 to find Ziklag destroyed and his wives Abigail and Ahinoam kidnapped.[18] Moreover, his men are very upset with him because their families have been endangered due to David's poor leadership.[19] In the midst of this, 1 Samuel 30:6 says, "David strengthened himself in the LORD his God." David, after strengthening himself in the Lord, shows what a repentant Christian looks and behaves like: He graciously led his people and gave back to those who helped him during his self-imposed exile.[20]

When we read that David "strengthened himself in the LORD his God," it means that, by faith alone, David laid hold of the Lord and his promises of salvation. Instead of self-reliance, David sought the counsel of Abiathar the High Priest after he repented.[21] As Christians today, we read and study Scripture to strengthen ourselves in the Lord. Like David, when we are strengthened in the Lord, we do not become self-reliant, but rather we delight in the Lord and do life with his people in our local churches.

To strengthen ourselves in the Lord means we remind ourselves of what Scripture says about God and his promises.

---

[17] 1 Samuel 28:2.
[18] 1 Samuel 30:3–5.
[19] 1 Samuel 30:6.
[20] 1 Samuel 30:20-31.
[21] 1 Samuel 30:7.

By doing so, we bring to bear biblical truth on the situation(s) we are faced with so that we might worship and delight in the Lord in and through those challenging situations. Amid such challenging situations, we may not always feel like reading or studying the Word. Like David, we often listen to the voice of our circumstances instead of the voice of faith from the Word, which tells us that the Lord is sufficient for every trial.[22]

As we are strengthened in the Lord, we will worship the Lord rightly, as he has prescribed in his Word, by delighting in his Word and growing in grace. Then we will be able to share the grace of God and be gracious with others because, like David, we are being strengthened in the Lord. Next let's consider together why we should memorize and meditate on the Word of God.

---

[22] 2 Corinthians 12:7–10.

3

Memorizing & Meditating
on the Word

I played tennis, soccer, and a few other sports competitively from a young age, until about my sophomore year when I stopped and focused on golf. In high school, I was quite the athlete. I played football, golf, tennis, and I worked out all the time in the gym. I think at one point I was even in several P.E. classes. I was a "gym rat." When I wasn't in the gym, I ran for fun everywhere or rode my bike. I was in excellent shape.

Just as cardio and strength training were imperative to my fitness as an athlete, memorizing and meditating on the Word of God is imperative to our spiritual fitness as Christians. Bible memorization and meditation are as necessary to our lives as breathing, eating, or working out. The Lord, through his trustworthy and reliable Word, has enabled the people of God to memorize and meditate on the Word in order to discipline ourselves for the sake of godliness.[1] Much like how you might go to the gym or for a walk to stay in shape, Paul is telling us in 1 Timothy 4:7–8 that we are to do the same in our walk with God. We are to discipline and train ourselves for the sake of godliness. Physical training, he says, has "some value," but "godliness is of value in every way, as it holds promise for the present life and also for the life to come."[2] Paul is saying that effort in spiritual discipline is of value not only because it holds promise

---

[1] 1 Timothy 4:7–8.
[2] 1 Timothy 4:7–8.

here today, but also because it holds promise in the life to come, in eternity.

Grace-driven effort in the Christian life

The Christian life is described as one of grace-fuelled effort.[3] If you were to look at the structure of Paul's epistle to the Ephesians, Paul considers in the first three chapters what is called "the indicative" (what Christ has done), and only then how the indicative fuels "the imperative" (what Christ commands us to do) in chapters four through six. We do not merit salvation, we do not grasp salvation by ourselves, and we do not exert the effort for our own sake. Instead, it is only by grace alone, through faith alone, in Christ alone that we are saved, held secure, and can pursue any grace-driven effort or discipline.

Dr. Martyn Lloyd-Jones is correct when he says:

> It is grace at the beginning, and grace at the end. So that when you and I come to lie upon our death beds, the one thing that should comfort and help and strengthen us there is the thing that helped us in the beginning. Not what we have been, not what we have done, but the grace of God in Jesus Christ our Lord. The Christian life starts with grace, it must continue with grace, it ends with grace. Grace wondrous grace. By the grace of God I am what I am. Yet not I, but the Grace of God which was with me.[4]

As we consider Paul's call in 1 Timothy 4 to train ourselves in godliness, we must think of this discipline as a grace-driven effort, from beginning to end. And the strategies laid out

---

[3] 1 Timothy 4:6–8; 2 Peter 1:5–10.
[4] D. Martyn Lloyd-Jones,. *Spiritual Depression: Its Causes and Cure* (Grand Rapids: Eerdmans, 1965), 52.

in the Word for this training in godliness are a means of grace to help us in our striving.

When theologians use the language of the "means of grace," what they mean is that these means are meant to help us grow in the grace and knowledge of the Lord Jesus.[5] The *means of grace* are not the beginning cause of our salvation. Instead, they help propel us forward in grace, relying and trusting on Christ from beginning until the end. The Christian, Paul says, is to consider discipline in their walk with God of *vital importance*.[6] It is so vital, in fact, that he says (in verse 7), "it holds promise for the present life and also for the life to come."[7] The same grace that saves you as a Christian is training you to renounce ungodliness[8] so that you can grow in the grace and knowledge of the Lord Jesus[9] and train yourself for godliness.[10] We engage in memorizing and meditating on the Scriptures because of the grace of God, which we have received because of the finished and sufficient work of Jesus.

Memorizing the Word
We are talking about memorizing the Word given by God, which is inspired and profitable for your very soul. Your very soul needs the Word for life and sustenance. You were created by God *for God*, and as such, only what God provides will truly satisfy you and bring lasting hope and fruit to your life. Memorizing the Word of God is precious when we see memorization, not as a duty to perform to get points in the eyes of God, but as

---

[5] 2 Peter 3:18.
[6] 1 Timothy 4:8.
[7] 1 Timothy 4:8.
[8] Titus 3:5.
[9] 2 Peter 3:16–18
[10] 1 Timothy 4:6–7

valuable because we are hiding the Word of God in our hearts and minds.[11]

When Scripture is stored in your heart and mind, it is available for the Holy Spirit to bring to your attention when you are tempted, facing a trial, dealing with a difficult person, or when you are counseling someone. The memorization of Scripture allows your mind easier access to the voice of God to come to mind and speak through you.

One practical reason memorizing is so essential is in the area of spiritual warfare. This is expressed in Ephesians 6:17, which says, "And take the helmet of salvation, and the sword of the Spirit, which is the word of God." When those whispers of Satan come your way—and they will come—remind yourself of Scripture. Do not believe those lies! Fight those lies with the Word of God! I recall a good friend once telling me, "Dave, you are fighting a battle that you were never meant to win because it's already been won!" As a Christian, you are in a war that has already been won by your Redeemer. You memorize Scripture to bring to mind the Word in the moment of temptation and challenge, so the Sword of the Spirit can be brought to bear in that situation. Jesus, when tempted in the wilderness, knew the Word and was therefore able to quote Scripture accurately amidst temptation.[12] Likewise, Christians ought to memorize Scripture so that it's available to the Holy Spirit to use and inflame our souls amid the daily struggles of life.

Memorizing Scripture not only enables us to wield its truth in our own lives, but it helps Christians to genuinely know the Word of God so that they can share it with others.

---

[11] Psalm 119:11.
[12] Matthew 4:1–11.

When you go to an ATM, you insert your debit card, enter your PIN, and select how much cash you want to withdraw. In a similar way, Scriptural memory is putting the Bible into our hearts and minds and then typing in the PIN when we are faced with temptation or challenges; this allows us to "withdraw" the deposit of the Word through biblical memorization. The more we deposit the Scriptures into our hearts and minds, the more stored Scripture we will have to pull up into our lives and deposit into the lives of others. As one friend of mine says, "How much of the Bible can you access?" By that he means, "How much of the Bible do you honestly know?" It's a convicting question and gets to the heart of why we should commit ourselves to memorizing Scripture: so we have timely and biblical advice to give to others that builds them up in the Word of God.

Memorization fuels meditation

One of the best reasons for memorizing the Scriptures is so that it fuels biblical meditation. When we memorize a verse of Scripture, we can meditate on it anytime, day or night. Psalm 119:97 says, "Oh, how I love your law! It is my meditation all the day."

In Joshua 1:8, we see the connection between success and the practice of meditation. Genuine success is not granted to those who stare off into space, but instead to those who stare deep into the Word of God. Biblical meditation invites Christians into the world of God in his Word, where real refreshment and joy begins. Every Christian who wants to grow in grace meditates on the Word and thinks deeply on the Word of God. The fruit of biblical meditation is action.[13] As we hear, read,

---

[13] Psalm 39:3.

study, and memorize the Word, the power of Scripture, fueled by biblical meditation, inflames and enlarges our soul. The more we engage in biblical meditation, the more we see the Word giving off its heat onto us, illuminating its truth to us through the Holy Spirit, whose Word provides insight and understanding, resulting in a passion for obedience to God by his grace. Thomas Watson pointedly notes, "The reason we come away so cold from reading the Word is because we do not warm ourselves at the fire of meditation."[14]

Biblical meditation is where we fill our minds with God's truth and where our hearts and minds are enflamed with a passion for God. As George Mueller said, "The vigor of our spiritual life will be in exact proportion to the place held by the Bible in our life and thoughts."[15] Mueller is right: how we view the Bible affects what we do with the Bible. It's what we do with the Word of God and how we view it and believe it that will lead to having the right actions in light of biblical truth. And that's why hearing, reading, and studying the Bible is so essential and also why biblical meditation is so critical. These are lifelong pursuits; eternal things. So, we press on and grow because, if we have the right view of the Bible itself, then we'll hold it in the right place in our hearts, thoughts, and lives.

Biblical meditation & the promises of God
What we think about reveals what we delight in. As a Christian, your life in Christ thrives best when your head and heart are in

---

[14] Thomas Watson, "How We May Read the Scriptures with Most Spiritual Profit," in *Puritan Sermons* (1674; reprint, Wheaton, IL: Richard Owen Roberts, 1981), 2:62. See also Thomas Watson, *Meditation: A Christian on the Mount*, ed. Dustin Benge (Peterborough: H&E Publishing, 2021).

[15] As attributed to George Mueller.

the soil of God's Word. It is in biblical meditation that we can soak up the water of the Word of God.[16]

Growing up in Seattle, I saw what happens when it rains hard—and by hard I'm talking a torrent of rain for several hours. Like the rains in Seattle, the Lord, through his Word, promises to take the Scriptures and bring them home into the soil-bed of our hearts. Without absorbing the Word of God, it will run off as rain runs into the drain after it downpours in Seattle.

Biblical meditation is one means of grace the Lord uses to help Christians be productive and fruitful servants of God. Biblical meditation is critical in our times when we face a torrent of information each day, because it helps Christians to be shaped by the Word and to grow in the grace of God. The Lord desires to take his Word and plant it deep into our hearts and lives, and one way he does this is through biblical meditation. The fruit of biblical meditation is a growing maturity in Christ.

Praying the Word
Integral to meditating on the Word is praying through the Word.[17] As Psalm 119:18 tells us, "Open my eyes that I may see wonderful things in your life." John 14:26 tells us that the Holy Spirit guides the Christian into all truth of the Scriptures. Meditation is more than merely concentration or mental energy being exerted for exertion's sake. Rather, we ought to pray and ask for illumination (to open our understanding to the Scripture), because doing so intensifies spiritual perception.

---

[16] Ephesians 5:26.
[17] For a helpful and concise book on prayer, see John Calvin, *Prayer: The Chief Exercise of Faith*, ed. Dustin Benge (Peterborough: H&E Publishing, 2020).

The Bible was written under the inspiration of the Holy Spirit. So, pray for the Holy Spirit to expand your understanding of the text, so that you can rightly understand it as you meditate on the Word. Praying over Scripture is an invitation for the Holy Spirit to hold his divine light over the text to show you what you cannot see without him. Consider, for example, why you would turn the light on in a room. Without the light switch turned on, you cannot see in the room. The Holy Spirit illuminates the Scripture so the lights "turn on" to help you see what you were unable to perceive without his gracious guidance in Scripture.

Conclusion

Memorizing the Scriptures allows us to store up God's truths in our hearts and minds and meditation is deep thinking on biblical truth, which defines biblical reality. Christian meditation is linked with prayer to God and responsible Holy Spirit-filled human action to bring about genuine transformation by the grace of God. Biblical Christian meditation is possible because of the grace of the Lord, who we can trust because he is wholly good, trustworthy, righteous, loving, and just in all his ways. The purpose of memorizing and meditating on the Word of God is for the sake of proper application.

Perhaps you can't possibly add another moment of your time to Scripture reading and memorization; I get it and I understand. Take what time you do have to spend in the Word and focus it. Read less, but use a more focused method to read, study, memorize, and meditate on the Word. The truth is, you can meditate any time on the Word (there is no specific minute or hour). Unlike how we need sleep as finite creatures, the

Lord is infinite and doesn't need time to sleep.[18] The best time to encounter the Word of God occurs as we are reading and delighting in him.

Now that we've considered this subject at some length, let's turn and discuss the vital issue of applying the Word of God, along with benefits and methods for doing so, in chapter four of this book.

---

[18] Isaiah 40:28.

4

Applying God's Word:
A Guide to Benefits & Methods

It was a conversation I will never forget. At the time, we were new to the church, and I was drawn to seek mentorship from one of the pastors at the church. He was a more seasoned Christian and had been in pastoral ministry for a long time. From very early on in my Christian walk, I've been drawn to being discipled by older men—wanting to learn from them and grow from their knowledge and experience.

While my desire was good and right, I was wrong in my approach with one of the pastors. Rather than waiting patiently to talk with him, I would interrupt conversations on Sunday (a pastor's busiest day of the week) by inserting myself into the conversation, which resulted in the person he was talking with walking away from the conversation they were having with him. One day he said we needed to talk and invited me to play golf with him, so I did.

I had arrived at church early for our time together and was excited to get to know one of my pastors. Well, as we drove from the church to the golf course, he said, "Can I tell you something?" Immediately that feeling you get when you know you're in trouble welled up within the pit of my stomach. I thought, "Oh, great, what did you do now, Dave?" As he talked, it was like a father talking to a son; he was loving but firm, gracious but truthful. He said in the most caring and kind way he could, "Dave, you have a relational maturity problem." Later on, as we worked together over five years, he would tell me, "You don't have a knowledge problem; you have an application problem." It took a lot of grace-fueled effort to address the issues going on in my life that caused me to lack patience, self-control, humility, and graciousness with others.

Application is a matter of obedience. The Holy Spirit desires to carry forth the Word you hear, read, study, memorize, and meditate on, and plant it deep within your heart. Here in California, we have the Redwood forests, and if you go there you will see substantially massive trees. These trees have significant root structures and are firmly planted in the soil. What God wants for you is for your heart and life to be grounded deep in the fertile soil of God's Word, so that you may experience transformation in every sphere of your life.

The benefits of applying the Word

The Word of God promises that God blesses those who apply it. James 1:22–25 is a definitive biblical text on integrating the Word of God into our lives, because he takes the problem head-on and helps us to resolve it. See, the Word of God both cuts[1] and brings healing, through repentance resulting in greater trust and growth in the grace of the Lord Jesus.[2]

James 1:22–25 says:

> But be doers of the Word, and not hearers only, deceiving yourselves. For if anyone is a hearer of the Word and not a doer, he is like a man who looks intently at his natural face in a mirror. For he looks at himself and goes away and at once forgets what he was like. But the one who looks into the perfect law, the law of liberty, and perseveres, being no hearer who

[1] Hebrews 4:12.
[2] 2 Peter 3:18.

forgets but a doer who acts, he will be blessed in his doing.

As we look at James 1:22-25, it's essential to consider what we've learned so far, as we talked about *hearing* the Word (chapter 1) and *doing* the Word[3] due to the implanted Word of the gospel in our lives.[4] The only reason we can look at the mirror and not fall into the pit of despair is because of the implanted Word of Christ through the Spirit in our lives. Similar to what James says in verses 1:22-25 is what Jesus says in John 13:17: "If you know these things, blessed are you if you do them."

James 1:22-25 helps make sure we do not get deceived, thinking all is well and not looking at ourselves with clarity. I can say I love my wife, but if I don't treat her with loving words and actions, then that's not her reality. If I'm not doing the little things, like saying loving things and doing loving actions, she is right to question my love of her. If I don't listen to her attentively, she will rightly feel that I don't care for her.

Similarly, if I *do* love her and show her that by paying attention to her words and engaging with them, I am showing her that I value her as a person. My love of my wife is not just something that I *think*, but I love her in real-time and with practical actions so she can not only perceive it, but it is her reality.

The Holy Spirit is at work in the life of the Christian to help them see and know Jesus.[5] According to James, we might know the truth powerfully, and it can be as plain as day as when you see yourself in the mirror.[6] As James says, if the Word is

---

[3] James 1:21.
[4] James 1:21.
[5] John 14:26; John 16:7-8.
[6] James 1:22-24.

not being driven down deep into the soil bed of our lives, we are like a man who looks in the mirror and then forgets immediately what he saw after he looks away.[7] James' point is that the one who is blessed by God is not the one who looks in the mirror and walks away unaffected, but the one who looks in the mirror with the Word and walks away transformed by looking to Jesus. Such a person is one whose life is going to be transformed and who is growing in grace; whose character is growing in godliness and who is going to be used powerfully by the Lord.

The Word "doers" in James 1:22 is *active*. Growing up, I remember my mom repeatedly saying, "Actions speak louder than words." The point James is making is similar to the one my mom made, but more forceful: "Become a doer." James is concerned that believing the right things should lead to right practice, for faith must lead to action.[8] James says that those who are genuinely wise are those who show it through evidence.[9] To those who know the right things and don't do them, James says that it is sin.[10]

And this is why I need you and you need me, within the context of our local churches. Above all else, we need to be hearing, reading, studying, memorizing, and meditating on the Word of God, because it contains the real diagnosis and the right remedy to our sin in the grace of God. In the local church, we can come alongside one another, encouraging one another in the faith and walking out our faith day-to-day by the strength the Holy Spirit provides. When we look in the "mirror" of the Word of God, the Holy Spirit comes alongside the Scriptures

---

[7] James 1:22–24.
[8] James 2:14–26.
[9] James 3:13.
[10] James 4:17.

44

to bring it to bear on our lives, resulting in conviction and confession of sin.[11]

Look in the mirror to Christ

Rather than gazing at ourselves carelessly, we must stare into the mirror of the Word of God and allow it to expose our sin. To profit from the Word of God as a mirror, we must understand what James is saying in James 1:25: "But the one who looks into the perfect law, the law of liberty, and perseveres, being no hearer who forgets but a doer who acts, he will be blessed in his doing."

The point James is making is powerful because the law of God is perfect, and since it is perfect, it is perfectly suited to guide our lives in this world. Remember, the law we are referring to here is the Law of Moses, the commands of the Prophets, and the example of godly conduct from the Old Testament children of God that illustrate holy living, which is ultimately fulfilled by Christ. James is helping his readers to take the Word and plant it, like a tree planted in good soil. He wants his readers to know not only the answer to the question of whether the gospel has saved your soul, but also whether you are presently preserving with joy in the goodness of God. And so, he commands that if the Word is implanted in you, then it will bring forth evidence that demonstrates it. Even though we stand in Christ who has fulfilled the law, James knows that obedience to the law's mirror of holy living is not a trivial issue.

James' point throughout his epistle isn't to suggest that the gospel is faith plus works, but that true and saving faith demonstrates itself because of the implanted Word.[12] Paul's

---

[11] John 16:6–8; 1 John 1:9.
[12] James 1:24.

point in Ephesians 2:8–10 is the same as James', but they come
at it from different directions. Paul is saying that we were once
dead in our trespasses and sins, but now we are made alive to
God by grace alone through faith alone in Christ alone.[13] It's
now by grace alone through faith alone in Christ alone that
Christians are "his workmanship, created in Christ Jesus for
good works, which God prepared beforehand, that we should
walk in them."[14]

James' point is the same as Paul's because, as we've seen
in this chapter, he's focused on how the implanted Word
saves,[15] and it's because of that Word that we can do good
works.[16] All of our good works, according to Paul and James,
are evidence that genuine saving faith in Christ has taken
place.[17] The source of obedience isn't our effort, our merit, or
what I'll do or not do, but the grace of God in Christ.[18] All
Christian obedience is rooted in the grace of God, which provides fuel for our loving God out of gratitude for the grace of
God.[19] All of this is why James' call for visible obedience is unwavering, and the logic is profoundly penetrating because he
knows that such obedience may be out of reach right now,
which is why he says in James 1:5 to ask for wisdom and the
strength of the implanted Word.

People today talk about wanting to be free to do whatever
they want, but this isn't true freedom. If you have a hard, loving, and gracious conversation with someone about what is go-

[13] Ephesians 2:1–9.
[14] Ephesians 2:10.
[15] James 1:21.
[16] James 2:14–26.
[17] Ephesians 2:10; James 2:14–26.
[18] Ephesians 2:1–8; 1 Corinthians 15:1–10.
[19] John 8:31; 14:15; 14:21; 14:23–24; 15:10–15; 1 John 2:3; 3:22; 3:24; 5:3.

ing on in their lives and (over time) see that they aren't applying what you said, what do you do? Do you rejoice because they are struggling? Do you laugh at them? No! You are sad because you love and care for this person and want the best for them.

The law of liberty helps us understand the character of God at the heart level. The law of liberty is suited to address man's condition and to bring the remedy of the gospel to bear on all of life. When we look at the mirror of our souls with the Word of God, we can find genuine freedom and blessing, and know how to love each other.[20] The Holy Spirit uses the Word as a mirror to hold it up to our lives and convict our hearts.[21]

Practical guidance on applying the Word

In chapter three, we discussed memorization and meditation. Biblical meditation leads to application and obedience to the Word of God. When God instructed Joshua in Joshua 1:8 to meditate on the Word of God day and night, he said that the purpose was, "so that you may be careful to do everything written in it." The promise was, "then you will be prosperous and successful," meaning that it wouldn't be a result of meditation alone, but a result of God's blessing upon meditation on the Word, which results in application of the Word. That day when my former pastor and one of my best friends said to me, "You have an application problem," was a big wake up call to me. See, rather than just staring at the Word and then looking away, I got help in applying it. To get the help and hope you need, you are going to have to open up the Word and read it with a desire to learn about God: his ways, character, and the message contained in the gospel. As a Christian, you believe that the

---

[20] 1 John 3:11–24; 1 John 4:7.
[21] John 16:6–8.

Word of God is not mere words of men, but the very breath of God.[22] By approaching the Word in the right way, you will aim to apply it to your life. Meditation is not an end goal in and of itself, as we considered in the previous chapter, but a means of grace to help us grow spiritually and to drive the Word more in-depth into our hearts and lives. Meditation is fuel for application.

We live in an information age—from social media and news outlets to a number of other avenues—where we are inundated with it more than ever before. What we need most, however, is to stop and come to the fount of the Word of God, where God himself offers genuine refreshment for parched spirits and food for our hungry souls. If you do not apply the Word of God to your life, you can read, study, memorize, and meditate all day long and not profit from it ever. In meditating on the Word, your heart is warmed and purified by the grace of God; it fuels us like a car at a gas station, encouraging us into passionate action for the glory of God.

Psalm 119:15 says, "I will meditate on your precepts and fix my eyes on your ways." Through meditation, King David says he discerned the ways of God and how to be a doer of the Word. As you meditate on the Word, ask good questions of the biblical text. The more questions you ask and answer about a verse, the more you'll gain insight and heart-level understanding about how it applies to your life and the lives of others.

Discussing biblical mediation and application in the Christian life isn't meant to exhaust us and run us into the ground reading, studying, and doing more for Jesus. Instead, it's to find genuine rest in our union with Christ himself,[23] because

---

[22] 2 Timothy 3:16–17; 2 Peter 1:20–21.
[23] Matthew 11:28–30.

we are now his friends.[24] As friends of God, Christians have been summoned before the throne of the grace to know the God of Grace.[25] In the Upper Room Discourse in John 14–16, Jesus taught the disciples much about the Holy Spirit. Christians today need to understand that it is the Holy Spirit who grows the people of God in the Word of God so they may honor what Jesus says in John 15:14 and "do what I command you."

As you obey Jesus, dear Christian friend, you'll also begin to see that the Word of God is not just a mere book, but God's gift to help you to see connections between the Scriptures, our world, and the lives of others. Then you'll start to do what John Stott wrote about in *Between Two Worlds*, or what Augustine of Hippo talked about in *The City of God*—understanding that the Kingdom of God is both here, in the now, and yet also in the future. The Kingdom is here now because of the finished and sufficient work of Christ. Through local churches, God is building his Kingdom through his people. And yet his kingdom is of the future, when he will glorify the precious possession— the apple of his eye: his people—and they will be entirely clothed in the righteousness of the Lord Jesus.[26]

To get to know Christ (your friend), you need to crack open that Bible and get to the hearing, reading, studying, memorizing, meditating, and application of it. Men and women throughout Church history, whom the Lord has used most powerfully, are Word-centered, Word-shaped, and Word-practicing Christians. The Lord uses these men and women de-

---

[24] John 15:14.
[25] 1 Peter 5:10; Hebrews 4:14–16.
[26] Revelation 3:5; Revelation 19:14.

spite their fear, anxiety, or their ability to speak/write. God desires to take the Word and drive it deep into your heart and life so he may use you.

Before we wrap up this first section and move into the next portion of this book, let me ask you a question, "Are you a *doer* of the Word?" Like me, you may have read the Bible since age five or earlier. Or perhaps you've read it for 50 (or more) years. Then again, maybe you've just started. The question here is whether you are daily delighting in the God who has given you a book full of the very words of God, and now whether you are presently applying and obeying the Word daily in your life.

But my question isn't whether you read the Word or know it, my question is whether you are *applying* the Word of God and obeying it. Hearing, reading, studying, meditating, and memorizing the Word are all great, but they all fail, like a falling tree in the forest, without *application*. The great difficulty you see in applying the Bible is that we are naturally opposed to the authority of the Word of God, which testifies of Christ and thus tells us about how we may be saved and transformed by the grace of God in all of life. I need you, and you need me, so that we don't just look at the mirror—like I did when I was full of "all the right answers," but whose truths weren't affecting my life. I did not see, at that time of my life, how the Bible was not just for my head, but for all of my life. Now I do see this, and also, my great daily need of Christ and doing life with the people of God. In our local churches, we need one another—to do life with one another—so that we can go out into our various vocations as Word-shaped and Word-formed Christians, carrying forth the grace of God to others. It's to this subject that we turn to in the next section of this book, discovering what a healthy local church and church members look like as they submit to—and live life under—the authority of the Word of God together.

5

The Local Church
& the Word

***

Calvin & the call to Geneva

John Calvin is considered one of the primary influences of the Protestant Reformation. We cannot consider here in this chapter the entirety of his life, but I want to highlight one specific instance and the background to it. It's a well-known story, so if you've heard it before, may it encourage you and remind you of the central place the Word of God is to have in the local church.

In 1536, John Calvin decided to move to Strasbourg, which is located in southwest Germany. However, as the war between Francis I and Charles V raged on, it prevented him from going to Strasbourg. Instead, Calvin was forced to stay in Geneva, located in Switzerland, where he intended only to spend one night. Being in the city of Geneva, he was noticed by others as the author of his famous book, *The Institutes of Christian Religion*. One man that met him there was William Farel, a man who led the Protestant Reformation for ten years.

At this time in history, Geneva had recently voted to leave the Roman Catholic Church and become a Reformation city. Geneva was in need of a teacher who had well-formed convictions about Reformed theology. To that end, Calvin's arrival in Geneva was a working of the kindness of God. His arrival resulted in Farel (a passionate church leader) challenging Calvin to take the job of teaching the people in Geneva the Word of God. Since Calvin was resistant to the idea, Farel resorted to threatening Calvin with imprecatory prayers. Calvin reports this incident in his own words:

> Farel, who burned with an extraordinary zeal to advance the gospel, immediately strained every nerve to detain me. And after having learned that my heart was set upon devoting myself to private studies, for which I wished to keep myself free from other pursuits, and finding that he gained nothing by entreaties, he proceeded to utter an imprecation that God would curse my retirement, and the tranquility of the studies which I sought, if I should withdraw and refuse to give assistance, when the necessity was so urgent. By this imprecation I was so stricken with terror, that I desisted from the journey which I had undertaken.[1]

Calvin began his ministry in Geneva, first as a lecturer, then as a pastor. With Farel, Calvin started the task of bringing the life and practice of the Church in Geneva into submission to the Word of God. Among the reforms Calvin brought was the exercise of church discipline at communion, which didn't sit well with the well-known citizens of Geneva, many of whom were living sinful lives. All of this led to the crisis of Easter Sunday, April 23, 1538, when Calvin refused to administer Communion to the leading people in the congregation who were living in rebellion against God while professing faith in Christ. All of this caused tensions so great that Calvin and Farel were both forced to leave Geneva.

---

[1] John Calvin, *John Calvin's Bible Commentaries - Psalms 1–35* (North Charleston, SC: Jazzybee Verlag, 2016), 23.

Calvin in Strasbourg

Calvin moved to Strasbourg after being forced out of Geneva, where he intended to go two years earlier. But Calvin was not left alone to his work, nor left to retreat into his writing, which he wanted to do. Instead, through the kindness of God, Calvin met Martin Bucer, who insisted that Calvin must continue in pulpit ministry. Once again, Calvin was threatened, this time by Bucer, which resulted in Calvin becoming the pastor of nearly five hundred Protestant refugees from France.

While in exile in Strasbourg, Calvin was given freedom to write and he was enormously productive, writing his commentary on Romans and enlarging the work of his *Institutes of Christian Religion*. Even so, with Calvin's departure from Geneva, the Roman Catholic Church aimed to return to Geneva. Cardinal Jacopo Sadoleto wrote an open letter to the people, inviting them to return to Roman Catholicism after Calvin's departure. The leaders of Geneva appealed to John Calvin to respond, which he did with the reply to Sadoleto, which was a compelling defense of the glory of God in the gospel of grace. That response was later considered the greatest apologetic for the Reformation. Also, during this time, Calvin married his wife Idelette de Bure, a widow with two children.

Calvin called back to Geneva

After three joyous years of writing and ministry in Strasbourg, the church in Geneva wrote to Calvin asking for his return to their city to be the pastor. During his time away, the religious and political landscape had deteriorated significantly. Calvin had no desire to return, saying in a letter to Farel on March 29, 1540, "Rather would I submit to death a hundred times than to that cross, on which one had to perish daily a thousand times over."[2] He changed his mind later, realizing that he needed to be entirely committed to God, which resulted in him bowing to the will of God and returning to his pastorate in Geneva.

Calvin returned to Geneva on September 13, 1541, and immediately resumed his exposition of Scripture—right at the verse following the last one he had covered before his exile. Such a continuation was a bold statement of what place verse-by-verse sermons would hold in his ministry.

The need for corporate Bible reading

Calvin's example in the above story is significant. He did *not* yield one inch of his convictions, and the Lord blessed his efforts, using him to write books, preach sermons, reach people all over Europe and many other parts of the world. What Calvin understood was the central place of the Word of God in the ministry of the local church.

In the first chapter of this book, we briefly reviewed the corporate reading of the Word of God. Now we return to those points so we can understand the importance of why Calvin left Geneva, and why he returned to preach the very next verse. To understand these points, let's now consider four reasons why the public reading of Scripture is vital to the local church.

First, Christians are commanded to read the Bible publicly. 1 Timothy 4:13 says to "Devote yourself to the public reading." Paul is commanding church officers to read the Scriptures publicly to help the people of God learn to read and hear the whole counsel of God, which is what the people of God from the Early Church to the present day have always done.

---

[2] Jules Bonnett, *Letters of John Calvin* (Frankfurt: Outlook Verlag, 2018), 136.

Second, the Lord transforms the people of God through the Word of God. Romans 12:1–2 is a classic biblical text on this subject:

> I appeal to you therefore, brothers, by the mercies of God, to present your bodies as a living sacrifice, holy and acceptable to God, which is your spiritual worship. Do not be conformed to this world, but be transformed by the renewal of your mind, that by testing you may discern what is the will of God, what is good and acceptable and perfect.

Romans, like all of Paul's epistles, would have first been read aloud to the Christian Church at Rome. The phrase "transformed by the renewal of your mind" in Romans 12:2 is not only individual but corporate, since Paul's goal in the context of this epistle in Romans 12:1–15:13 is to give instructions on the practical outworking of the mercy of God as the people of God do life with one another. Corporately, through the preaching of the Word of God, the people of God are transformed by the grace of God, so they may worship him by offering their whole lives to him in adoration and praise.[3]

Third, the Bible was meant to be read aloud. Long before Scripture was spread through the written form, it was transmitted orally. The Greco-Roman culture was an oral culture, and literature in the ancient world was spoken. For example, while the New Testament epistles were written down, they would have been read aloud to the congregation and only then spread around to the other churches through the known world.

---

[3] Matthew 2:2; John 4:20; Acts 13:2; 1 Corinthians 14:25; Hebrews 12:28; 13:15–16; Revelation 11:1.

Lastly, hearing the Scriptures is different than reading it alone privately. I often listen to the Scriptures on the YouVersion app on my cell phone in the mornings while I'm getting ready for work. I find hearing the Word opens new vistas of biblical understanding for me, which helps me in my reading of the passages I'm listening to or reading that day. Hearing the Word and reading the Word are both critical, and both are equal in their importance. Hearing the Word, whether on the YouVersion app or read aloud in the local church, can help the people of God to receive the Word of God together. The 1689 *London Baptist Confession of Faith* is right when it says,

> The authority of the Holy Scripture, for which it ought to be believed, dependeth not upon the testimony of any man or church, but wholly upon God (who is truth itself), the author thereof; therefore it is to be received because it is the Word of God.[4]

Scripture as a community treasure

The four reasons listed above form the basis for seeing the Scriptures as a community treasure. Reading the Word in community need not be long-faced and doleful, but should come alive with the real personalities behind the words themselves. 1 Timothy 4:13 (ESV) says, "Until I come, devote yourself to the public reading of Scripture, to exhortation, to teaching."

Terry Johnson rightly explains, "What the Apostle Paul wants done in the corporate gathering of God's people is the public reading of Scripture. The practice of the Jewish synagogue was to unroll the scrolls of Scripture, read a portion,

---

[4] Bob L'Alonge, *General Bible Introduction & Articles of Faith: The Particular Baptist Historicist Understanding of the Sacred Scriptures Given by God to Mankind* (Lincoln, 2003), 95.

mark where they stopped, and then the next Sabbath pick up
again where they left off."⁵ He calls this reading *"Lectio Con-
tinua*," which he says is the "consecutive, sequential readings—not, by the way, *Lectio Selecta* readings, selected from
here or there."⁶ Authors Jim Scott Orrick, Brian Payne, and
Ryan Fullerton in *Encountering God Through Expository Preaching* explain that when church officers read the Bible well, "not
only will you help people to understand the Bible, you will also
help them to love the Bible and regard it for what it is—the
Word of God."⁷

Terry Johnson helpfully explains,

> Jesus, in the synagogue in Nazareth,⁸ and the Apostle
> Paul, at Pisidian Antioch and elsewhere,⁹ provide ex-
> amples of this public discipline in action. The Apostle
> James also provides an explanation of the practice of
> the synagogue as well: "For Moses from ancient gen-
> erations has in every city those who preach him, since
> he is read in the synagogues every Sabbath."¹⁰

Johnson continues,

> If we are convinced that we are born-again by the liv-
> ing and abiding Word,¹¹ that we are sanctified by the
> truth,¹² and that our souls—as the Apostle Paul says

⁵ Johnson, "The Public Reading."
⁶ Johnson, "The Public Reading."
⁷ Jim Scott Orrick, Brian Payne and Ryan Fullerton, *Encountering God through
Expository Preaching: Connecting God's People to God's Presence Through God's Word*
(Nashville: B&H Academic, 2017), 124.
⁸ Luke 4:16–19.
⁹ Acts 13:15; 19:8.
¹⁰ Johnson, "The Public Reading."
¹¹ 1 Peter 1:23.
¹² John 17:17.

are "nourished on the words of the faith and of sound doctrine,"[13] we will require a prominent role in the public assembly for the Word of God; whether for our personal benefit or for the sake of the health and well-being of the whole Church.[14]

Listening to sermons in church

Now that we have some idea of why Calvin was so committed to verse-by-verse preaching, and why it's so central to the life and health of the local church, let's discuss how we are to "sit under" a sermon. After all, it's wonderful to hear the Word preached, but we need to be doers of the Word, not merely hearers.[15]

Going to church each Sunday and sitting under godly, loving, biblical, and practical preaching, week in and week out, should be enjoyed as a privilege by God's people. While some people, like myself, learn best by sitting and listening, I know many people get more out of sermons by taking notes. When I'm listening to a sermon, I try to always do the following three things:

1. Open my Bible and follow along as the pastor preaches the Word;
2. Listen for critical ideas and points;
3. Learn to interpret the biblical text from the pastor/preacher's example.

Open your Bible

---

[13] 1 Timothy 4:6
[14] Johnson, "The Public Reading."
[15] James 1:22–25.

First, open your Bible and follow along as the pastor teaches the Word. Whether you have a Bible app on your phone, or you have a physical copy of God's Word, always be sure to have your Bible open so you can follow along as the pastor is preaching. Paul commended the Bereans,[16] because they checked to see if what he was saying was biblical, and the Thessalonians, for how they received the Word of God.[17]

As Christians, we should be known for our love for God.[18] A real love for God will produce a love for his Word, his people, and his Church.[19] We are living in a time when biblical illiteracy is on the rise. By opening your Bible during the week on your own, at Bible study, and on Sunday at your local church, you can grow in your knowledge, understanding, and application of God's Word.[20] This is why following along as your pastor preaches the Word is so important—it will help you see what your pastor sees in the text, which will help you to learn how to read the Bible well on your own.[21]

Listen for key ideas & points

Some pastors provide an outline/notes for you to follow during the sermon. If this is the case, I encourage you to follow along with the outline (and fill it in, if applicable) as the pastor preaches. This outline is a crucial tool to help you take notes. If the pastor does not provide an outline, however, it is a good practice to create one of your own (or make basic notes) during the sermon.

---

[16] Acts 17:11.
[17] 1 Thessalonians 2:13.
[18] Matthew 22:37–40.
[19] Matthew 22:37–40; Ephesians 5.
[20] 2 Timothy 2:15.
[21] 2 Timothy 2:15.

DAVE JENKINS

While you're listening to the sermon, look for critical ideas; they may be points the pastor brings out in his sermons, or they may be thoughts brought to mind by the Holy Spirit. These are valuable insights to write down because they may encourage you or others later in the week or further down the road.

As a Bible teacher, sometimes I'll repeat something a few times to help the listener understand how critical it is to the whole message. Those key ideas may be the ones the pastor mentions, but they may also be something else in the passage that is helpful to you. You never know when those thoughts will have an impact later on and how they can be used by the Lord to minister to others.

Learn to interpret the text from your Pastor's example
One of the main objectives for faithful verse-by-verse preaching is that, week after week and year after year, people get to see how the pastor reads, understands, and interprets the biblical text. This is one of the primary reasons why verse-by-verse expository preaching is so relevant.

As Christians, we should be known for handling the Word of God well.[22] The faithful pastor preaches the biblical text to help people see how he got the points he did from the biblical text under consideration. In other words, the faithful pastor exegetes the biblical text to help the people of God see what the passage teaches, by drawing it out in helpful ways so people can learn to interpret the biblical texts themselves. Orrick, Payne, and Fullerton explain that the purpose of this is because, "genuine passion grows out of understanding the truth. The most crucial factor in becoming a good reader of Scripture is to have

---

[22] 2 Timothy 2:15.

a good understanding of what you are reading."²³ The goal of verse-by-verse preaching is to help Christians love the Lord of the Word, to grow in the knowledge of the Word, so they can become more like Jesus by learning to discern the Word of God rightly.²⁴

Maybe you've never considered listening intentionally to a sermon or note-taking. In every sermon, there will be points that you'll find more helpful than others. I encourage you to listen well, and take notes if you want, whether that's on an outline provided, a notebook you bring (or other note-taking device), or just mentally (although, let that method be a last resort). As you do so, you'll find that you will remember more of the sermons you hear.

Listening well and taking quality notes during the sermon is a means to an end. That end is our growth in Christ and understanding of the Bible.²⁵ You leave church each week sent out on a mission by God to make disciples of the nations for the glory of God.²⁶ Listening well to what is being taught to you with an open Bible, while jotting down key ideas and watching how your pastor interprets the Bible, will help you to grow in your knowledge and application of the Bible.²⁷ This will in turn help you to grow in the grace of God.²⁸

Love the Lord & one another
In 2 John 1:4-6, John writes, "I rejoiced greatly to find some of your children walking in the truth, just as we were commanded

---

²³ Orrick, Payne and Fullerton, *Encountering God through Expository Preaching*, 126.
²⁴ Matthew 22:37-40; Romans 8:28-30; 2 Timothy 2:15; 2 Peter 3:18.
²⁵ 2 Timothy 2:15.
²⁶ Matthew 28:18-20; Mark 16:15; Luke 24:46-48; John 20:21; Acts 1:8.
²⁷ James 1:22-25; 2 Timothy 2:15.
²⁸ 2 Peter 3:18.

by the Father. And now I ask you, dear lady—not as though I were writing you a new commandment, but the one we have had from the beginning—that we love one another. And this is love, that we walk according to his commandments; this is the commandment, just as you have heard from the beginning, so that you should walk in it."

John's point here is relevant to our discussion about listening to sermons because his goal is for the people of God to "walk in the truth just as we were commanded by the Father"[29] so that they would love one another. The "walking in the truth"[30] mentioned by John here carries with it living in a manner pleasing to the Lord. The "commandments" they have "heard from the beginning"[31] must constantly steer the life of the people of God, so they are guided by and display the love of God to one another and others.[32] At the outset of 2 John, John uses the word "truth"[33] because Christians are to be in close communion with Jesus, who is the truth.[34] Christians are to be people of the Word and to be shaped by the Word so they will be able to spot counterfeits and deceivers.[35]

This week I encourage you to pick up and read, study, and apply the Bible to your life,[36] so you can "know the truth because the truth abides in us and will be with us forever."[37] The person and work of the Lord Jesus are the foundation upon which the Christian life and ministry are to be grounded.

---

[29] 2 John 4.
[30] 2 John 4.
[31] 2 John 5.
[32] John 13:35.
[33] 2 John 1.
[34] John 14:6.
[35] 2 John 7–11.
[36] Psalm 1:2–3; Jeremiah 15:6; James 1:22–25.
[37] 2 John 1–2.

The content of the gospel according to John in 2 John 1:3 is, "grace, mercy, and peace will be with us, from God the Father and from Jesus Christ the Father's Son, in truth, and love."[38] One of the primary fruits of such love for the content of gospel truth is love, which is echoed by Paul and Peter, who join truth with love.[39] By growing in love for biblical truth, every Christian will grow in love for the Lord and others around them.[40] The goal of all this is to hunger and thirst for the righteousness which Jesus alone provides in his finished and sufficient work, which is why Christians aren't only concerned with listening to a sermon well, but with consistently applying their growth in the grace and knowledge of the Lord Jesus.[41]

We are only getting started on this topic. As you turn the page to the next chapter, prepare yourself to explore more about why you sit under sound biblical sermons. There you'll discover the pastor's responsibility to preach the Word of God, as well as church members' responsibility to hear, heed, and obey the Word preached as they live in community with one another.

[38] 2 John 1:3–4.
[39] Ephesians 4:15; 1 Peter 1:22.
[40] Matthew 22:37–40.
[41] 2 Peter 1:3–10.

6

THE LOCAL CHURCH
& THE PREACHING OF THE WORD

It was a conversation I never thought I would need to have within the confines of a local church, but here I was having it nonetheless. A man had told me and one of the other pastors from our church, "I don't need to hear the Word preached on Sunday. I come for the fellowship." Alarming issues were showing up in this man's life, as is usually the result when one does not see the need to be a part of the corporate gathering of the local church and for the Word to be rightly preached. To that end, one of my pastors and I attempted to come alongside and help him to understand his need for the preaching of the Word and the corporate gathering of the people of God.

When I was in seminary, I would often sit in coffee shops with a pile of theology books on my table. As I worked on my homework, I would often be asked, "What are you studying?" This would provide a perfect opening to share with others what I was reading, thinking about, or writing on. Often in these conversations, the person would tell me how they are having Bible study at this coffee shop, while pointing in the direction of said study at another table. When I asked what church they attended, the answer was often disconcerting—they didn't attend any, but rather the Bible study itself was what they considered to be their "church." In fact, I rarely received a response indicating that the person attended a nearby church regularly.

What all of these people failed to understand is the purpose that the Lord has for the corporate gathering of the Church. On the Lord's Day, the Lord gathers his people to hear his Word preached, to worship, and participate in the sacraments (baptism and communion). Some Christians suggest they don't need to attend church, but even among those who do know they need it, they believe they don't need the sermon because they've moved past that "stage" of their Christian life.

To be clear, there are many reasons why people stop attending church, and I've personally experienced them all, including spiritual abuse by pastors and ministry leaders. However, I never quit faithfully attending the church during these seasons of life but continued in faithful church attendance each Lord's Day. Additionally, I understand very well why some people feel that there is only hypocrisy in the church, but we don't sit under the preached Word of God from perfect men. The qualifications for a pastor/elder do not talk about a "perfect man." There is only one perfect God-Man, and that is *Christ alone.*[1] Even so, the biblical qualifications do matter, as listed in 1 Timothy 3:1–7 and Titus 1:5–8, because they are Paul's expectation of what a normal Christian life looks like, and what is expected of a Christian in regards to how they are to live.

Jesus' use of Scripture in preaching

Jesus engaged in what is known today as *expository preaching,* which is preaching the point of the text as the primary point of the sermon. We should observe how frequently Jesus' teaching

---

[1] John 19:4; 2 Corinthians 5:21; Hebrews 2:16–18; 4:14–16; 1 Peter 2:22; 1 John 3:5; 1 Timothy 2:5–6.

involves the exposition of Scripture. When Jesus began his ministry in the synagogue of Nazareth, he started with a reading from the prophet Isaiah:

> And he came to Nazareth, where he had been brought up. And as was his custom, he went to the synagogue on the Sabbath day, and he stood up to read. And the scroll of the prophet Isaiah was given to him. He unrolled the scroll and found the place where it was written, "The Spirit of the Lord is upon me because he has anointed me to proclaim good news to the poor. He has sent me to proclaim liberty to the captives and recovering of sight to the blind, to set at liberty those who are oppressed, to proclaim the year of the Lord's favor." And he rolled up the scroll and gave it back to the attendant and sat down. And the eyes of all in the synagogue were fixed on him. And he began to say to them, "Today this Scripture has been fulfilled in your hearing."[2]

It was Jesus' custom, his regular habit, to read the Word of God. Here, he starts with the Word and then moves on to explain its meaning, ultimately pointing to himself.

Again, Jesus' great "Bread of Life" sermon, found in John 6:32–59, involved the explanation of the Bible's teaching on manna that came through Moses. Even though Jesus could impress his hearers by performing miracles, he still rested the authority of his teaching on the truth of the Scriptures. It is *vital* that Bible preachers preach with authority today, and this can come only by faithfully presenting the truth of God's Word.[3] It is because of the authority of the Bible as God's revealed Word

---

[2] Luke 4:16–21.
[3] 2 Timothy 3:16.

that the Puritan Thomas Watson could say, "In every sermon preached, God calls to you, and to refuse the message we bring, is to refuse God himself."[4]

Church members need good preaching

Preaching is vital to the health and growth of the Church and the Christian life. Jesus used Scriptures to teach us how we are to live our lives.[5] Jesus exercised his teaching ministry to confront the religious people who thought they had it all figured out.[6] He also preached to the crowds and called people to himself.[7] Jesus divided the audience between those who believed and those who remained in their unbelief.[8]

The preaching of the Word of God can either soften or harden our hearts. One of the clearest signs of the Holy Spirit at work in the life of the believer is a hunger and thirst for God's Word.[9] Yes, you should be reading your Bible daily, but you should also be seeking to apply that Word into your life.[10]

The same principle applies when hearing a sermon. It's not enough to just *hear* the sermon, but it is a good *first step*. Now, heed it and apply the preached Word to your life.[11] Then your heart will be soft before the Lord, and you will walk uprightly before him.[12]

---

[4] Thomas Watson, *A Body of Practical Divinity in a Series of Sermons on the Shorter Catechism* (Mishawaka, IN: Palala Press, 2015), 201.

[5] Matthew 22:37–40.

[6] Matthew 23; Luke 11:37–54.

[7] John 12:32.

[8] John 6:64; 7:40–52; John 10:19.

[9] Matthew 5:6.

[10] Jeremiah 15:16; James 1:22–25.

[11] James 1:22–25.

[12] Psalm 15:2; 84:11; 1 Timothy 2:15.

The faithful preaching of God's Word helps us to grow to be like Christ.[13] It also helps us to grow in the knowledge of who God is and what he is like, what he commands us to do now, and the parameters of his mission—that is, seeking the lost and making disciples for his glory.[14] This is the reason why the argument that "we don't need sermons anymore because we've outgrown them" is the wrong one to make.

We need to sit under the faithful preaching of God's Word; preaching that considers the point of the passage as the point of the sermon. We need to sit under such preaching— teaching that not only takes seriously what the Bible says, but applies the biblical principles and makes a beeline to the finished and sufficient work of Jesus.[15] Such preaching will either harden our hearts (and confirm our unbelief) or soften them, bringing along with it the conviction of sin, repentance, and growth in godliness.[16] All of this is why preaching is essential to the Christian life.

Biblical preaching
At this point, you might agree that sitting under faithful preaching is important, but what does biblical preaching look like? Biblical preaching prayerfully preaches the gospel of Jesus Christ through the power of the Holy Spirit. To unpack the connection of preaching the Word, prayer, and the Holy Spirit, let's look to the preaching of Charles Spurgeon as an example.

---

[13] Romans 8:28-30.
[14] Luke 19:10; 2 Peter 3:18.
[15] John 5:39; Luke 24:27.
[16] John 16:3; 2 Peter 1:3-11; 3:18.

John Broadus, in his book, *On the Preparation and Delivery of Sermons*, stated that, "The ultimate requisite for the effective preacher is complete dependence upon the Holy Spirit."[17] Likewise, Bryan Chapell teaches that the biblical description of the Spirit's work challenges "all preachers to approach their task with a deep sense of dependence upon the Spirit of God."[18] There is little attention given to the Spirit in relationship to preaching and teaching today. Zachary Eswine explains that, "Spurgeon's intentional explicitness regarding the work of the Holy Spirit in preaching offers reasonable explorations into deeper caverns of intricacy, which may enable an infant theology on the Holy Spirit to take more steps."[19] Spurgeon believed that "the Spirit of God was precious to the people of God, and therefore sought to make the person and work of Christ the main focal point of his preaching and instruction to other preachers."[20]

The reason Spurgeon emphasized the work of the Spirit is because, as Jesus says in John 14:16–17, the Holy Spirit is the Spirit of Truth. Dr. Heisler explains, "The *Spirit of Truth* is sent by the Father, at the request of the Son, and indwells believers as a resident minister, who guides believers into all truth."[21] In John 16:13 Jesus describes the Holy Spirit as guiding Christians into biblical truth saying, "When the Spirit of truth comes, he will guide you into all the truth, for he will not speak on his own authority, but whatever he hears he will

[17] John Broadus, *On the Preparation and Delivery of Sermons*, 4th Edition, revised by Vernon L. Stanfield (San Francisco: Harper, 1979), 16.
[18] Bryan Chapell, *Christ-Centered Preaching: Redeeming the Expository Sermon* (Grand Rapids: Baker Books, 1994), 24.
[19] Zachary W. Eswine, *The Role of the Holy Spirit in the Preaching Theory and Practice of Charles Haddon* Spurgeon (Ph.D. diss. Regent University, 2003), 228.
[20] Quoted in Greg Heisler, *Spirit-Led Preaching* (Nashville: B&H Publishing, 2007), 126.
[21] Heisler, *Spirit-Led Preaching*, 54–55.

speak, and he will declare to you the things that are to come."
Biblical preachers prayerfully rely on the Spirit of Truth because it points believers to Jesus, who is the way, the truth, and
the life.[22]

Heisler explains:

> Jesus identified the Spirit's ministry as a continuation
> of his own ministry; in fact, John 14:16–18 makes it
> clear that the Holy Spirit is of the same kind (deity) as
> Jesus. The Spirit reveals and glorifies Christ by mag-
> nifying Christ's teaching, Christ's gospel, and
> Christ's work as the grand fulfillment of God's re-
> demptive plan. The Bible is united in its testimony to
> Jesus Christ, and the Spirit's joy is giving witness to
> this testimony to the people of God. Spirit-led preach-
> ing comes into alignment with the Spirit's ministry of
> glorifying Jesus Christ by proclaiming the written
> Word to glorify the living Word. Spirit-led preaching
> is the biblically defined ministry combined with the
> theological relationship between the Word and the
> Spirit. This combination demands Christ-centered
> preaching. The biblical and theological foundation for
> the Word and Spirit in preaching is seen in the fact
> that the Scriptures are Christ-centered, the Spirit is
> Christ-centered, and the preacher is to be Christ-cen-
> tered.[23]

Charles Spurgeon understood the importance of preaching the
Gospel in the power of the Holy Spirit, which is why he notes:

> The gospel is preached in the ears of all; it only comes
> with power to some. The power that is in the gospel

---

[22] John 14:6.
[23] Heisler, *Spirit-Led Preaching*, 126.

does not lie in the eloquence of the preacher; otherwise men would be converters of souls. Nor does it lie in the preacher's learning; otherwise it would consist in the wisdom of men. We might preach till our tongues rotted, till we should exhaust our lungs and die, but never a soul would be converted unless there were a mysterious power going with it the Holy Ghost changing the will of man. Oh Sirs! We might as well preach to stone walls as preach to humanity unless the Holy Ghost be with the Word to give it power to convert the soul.[24]

Biblical preachers, like Charles Spurgeon, act as the mouthpieces of God. They know that it is ultimately God who does the work, but they are called to faithfully preach his words to their hearers.

This true and whole dependence on God leads to humility. John Stott explains that "preachers must be humble in mind (submissive to the written Word of God), have a humble ambition (desiring an encounter to take place between Christ and His people), and a humble dependence (relying on the power of the Holy Spirit)."[25] Preachers must aim to be faithful to God's Word by lifting up the glory of Christ in the power of the Holy Spirit.[26] The confidence the preacher has must come from heartfelt knowledge of the Word of God by dwelling richly upon the Word, which is the Truth.[27] Only in this way will the preacher know the Truth he professes and be able to

---

[24] Charles Haddon Spurgeon, *Trumpet Calls to Christian Energy: A Collection of Sermons* (London: Passmore and Alabaster, 1875), 31.

[25] John Stott, *Between Two Worlds* (Grand Rapids: Wm. B. Eerdmans, 1982), 335.

[26] 2 Timothy 4:2.

[27] Colossians 3:16.

bear testimony about the cross in demonstration of Word and Spirit.[28]

Spurgeon's spirituality emerged from the Word of God. As Raymond Brown expressed it, "His spirituality was essentially a Biblical spirituality."[29] Spurgeon was a man deeply influenced by the Puritans who according to Lewis Drummond, "believed in a disciplined spirituality which to him meant the diligent, meditative study of the Scriptures."[30]

Faithful preaching & faithful listening

As we considered in chapter five with the example of John Calvin leaving Geneva and coming back only to pick up where he had stopped preaching, we need Bible preachers with the same focus and intensity as Calvin in our day. Our need, like in Calvin's day, is for the Word of God to be central in the life of the local church.

Expository preaching is the most faithful way of preaching because it reveals that the preacher believes that the Bible is reliable and trustworthy, so much so, that he grounds his sermons in the Word.[31] Expository preaching best articulates and helps God's people learn to read, study, and interpret the Word rightly.[32] Additionally, expository preaching alone addresses the significant issues of the day—including biblical illiteracy and false teaching.

---

[28] 1 Corinthians 1:18-31.

[29] Lecture given by Raymond Brown at the Celebration of Spurgeon's 150th anniversary of his birth at William Jewell College, Liberty, Missouri.

[30] Lewis Drummond, *Spurgeon Prince of Preachers* (Grand Rapids: Kregel, 1992), 573.

[31] What I have in mind by "reliable and trustworthy" here is that we believe that the Bible is inspired, inerrant, sufficient, clear, and authoritative.

[32] 2 Timothy 2:15.

No one can "outgrow" sitting under the faithful preaching of the Word of God because no one can outgrow the words that God has spoken to his people and no one can outgrow applying his Word to their life. It's through the preaching of the Word that God, by his Spirit, forms a people who were once not his people, and is conforming them into his image and likeness.[33] It's not only principally through preaching, which is the fuel God uses, but in small groups studying the Word, where the Word is being applied in the lives of his people. It's now time to consider the place and importance of small group Bible studies—gatherings where we study together and learn to "do life" together, submitted to the Word—that we turn to in our next chapter.

---

[33] Romans 8:28–20; 1 Peter 2:8–10.

7

THE IMPORTANCE OF SMALL GROUPS

Around the end of summer, at most local churches you might hear the call to join a small group and wonder, "What's that about?" I hope you ask that question, because it's an important one. A small group is typically comprised of about 10–20 people, with one person who leads the discussions and perhaps another who is the host/facilitator. Let's briefly consider three reasons why you should be in a small group.

Why participate in a small group?
First, we should be in a small group because we need to grow in our faith. Small groups are the place where we take what we learn on Sundays and put our Christianity to practice. In groups I've led, we share openly and ask questions of the text we're studying, along with the prepared questions. We discuss—often *intensely*—what the passage means or what issues it raises that we deal with in everyday life. This leads us to discuss the intersection of the Bible and daily life. Our discussions are often passionate, and opinions are made known on a wide variety of issues. We bring the mess of our lives in and deal with it together (even with people who we might not know all that well at first). We do all of this because we love one another, as brothers and sisters in Christ, and want to spur one another onto love and good works.[1]

Second, we need to be in a small group because we need accountability and prayer from fellow believers. Once, during

---

[1] Hebrews 10:24.

a small group session, I got a text from my mom regarding my dad, who has dementia. I was close to tears, and we stopped our study so I could explain what was going on. I read—word for word—what my mom said, and my response to her text message. While this doesn't happen frequently, I have to say it meant a lot to me that the group stopped and prayed for me. This is what small groups are about—a place where we take seriously what the Bible teaches and apply it in practical ways by caring for one another.

Thirdly, we need to be in a small group because we need one another's insights and perspectives. Everyone benefits in a small group when all the members participate. The amount of education we have is not essential, and we can all learn from one another (I'm a seminary-educated Christian, and I've been a believer since I was a little kid, and I greatly benefit from the insights and perspectives of the other people in my small group). We might think we've made up our minds on a particular issue, but healthy small group discussion can help us realize we haven't understood it from all sides (I've had that happen many times). We can open up and share what we really think about issues from the Bible, and then discover what the Word of God teaches. We can take what we learn and share it with others. Who wouldn't want to be a part of that?

Finally, small groups provide the ideal environment to really grow in our ability to interpret the Bible by paying close attention to context. One of the most critical aspects for sound biblical interpretation is understanding the context of the passage being considered. Think of the most exciting things your pastor says week in and week out in his sermon. You may even be astonished weekly by some interesting nugget he says in his sermon that you've never considered or observed before in the passage he's preaching on. You wonder, "How did he discover that?" Well, the truth is, he's done his homework and prepared well. But the key to his study is understanding the context; not just the immediate context of the passage (examining the surrounding verses/chapters), but also the culture (or time-period) of the writer. By taking the time to wrestle with a text with fellow believers in an open setting, we are able to grasp the Scriptures in a deep way with both our hearts and minds.

Hebrews 10:19-25 & the Christian life

God created us to be in relationship with himself *and* with others. Small group is all about growing together, providing accountability, and opening us up to new perspectives as fellow believers discuss the Word together. We desperately need this—we desperately need one another. The author of Hebrews emphasizes a believer's need for Christian community. In Hebrews 10:19-25, the author makes a transition from great doctrinal teaching to applying that doctrine to the life of his hearers and readers.[2] In the first part of this passage, the emphasis is on the confidence the Christian has in Christ, namely how they can draw near to God through the blood of Jesus by holding on and treasuring the sufficiency of Christ's work. The

---

[2] "Therefore, brothers, since we have confidence to enter the holy places by the blood of Jesus, by the new and living way that he opened for us through the curtain, that is, through his flesh, and since we have a great priest over the house of God, let us draw near with a true heart in full assurance of faith, with our hearts sprinkled clean from an evil conscience and our bodies washed with pure water. Let us hold fast the confession of our hope without wavering, for he who promised is faithful. And let us consider how to stir up one another to love and good works, not neglecting to meet together, as is the habit of some, but encouraging one another, and all the more as you see the Day drawing near" (Hebrews 10:19-25).

by-product of this is found in Hebrews 10:24–25, with the focus being on how Christians are to stir one another up to love and refrain from neglecting to meet with one another.

Christians spur one another on by praying for each other (by name) for the development of volitional, agape love and specific good deeds. Second, we are to "spur on" each other by living our lives as an example of the pursuit of holiness to others. Third, it is necessary to spur each other on through God's Word. The more we internalize the Word, allowing God's Word to flow through us, the more we will become conduits of its virtues and gentle examples and provokers of grace. Finally, we have to take responsibility to verbally spur each other on through words of encouragement, and do it all the more as you see the Day of the Lord approaching.

But it's not only in small groups that we need to "stir up" each other; we've been called to the mission of making disciples of Jesus in and through the local church. In the local church we gather around the Word, to study it and hear it preached, and then we scatter into our communities, neighborhoods, and cities so that we can make disciples of Jesus. In our next chapter, we will consider the Great Commission and how the commission of Jesus is to be fulfilled in and through local churches.

8

Distractions, the Local Church, and Making Disciples who Make Disciples

The Great Commission is an amazing truth that has a great deal of meaning for the Christian life. However, when our focus is only on making disciples rather than being a disciple who makes disciples, we can easily miss the main point: *discipleship*. The first obligation of Jesus' disciples is not to make more disciples, but to be followers of Jesus, who abide in him. In other words, the Great Commission is more than making disciples; it is also an entire lifestyle and worldview. It is only when we are abiding in Jesus and growing in him that we will engage in the work of the Great Commission.

Union with Christ & the Christian

In the Upper Room Discourse in John 15:1-15, Jesus tells his disciples they are to abide in him, which means to *remain* in him. But we cannot abide on our own. Just as it is vital for every car to have oil and gas for it to run, every Christian has a power supply. Thomas Goodwin, speaking of that power supply, said, "Being in Christ, and united to him, is the fundamental constitution of a Christian."[1] The power supply Jesus provides *is* union with Christ through the Holy Spirit. It is in union with Christ that we find our identity, meaning, value, and worth. What others need to see is this discipleship—Jesus forming in

---

[1] Thomas Goodwin, *Of Christ the Mediator* in *The Works of Thomas Goodwin*, ed. Thomas Smith (1861-1866; rep., Grand Rapids: Reformation Heritage Books, 2006), 5:350.

81

us as we grow in our service of him. Jesus, through his people, is how disciples are made.

The Point of parachurch ministry, the local church, and the Great Commission

It also needs to be said that the context and outworking of the Great Commission is primarily in and through the local church, and from there to the ends of the world. That is not to minimize parachurch ministries, or to say that they are "second class." In my work at Servants of Grace, I lead a multi-media ministry, but the goal of the ministry isn't to replace the local church, but to be a resource to the local church. It's been said that the local church is the hope of the world, which means that, since God ordains the local church, it is being sanctified by him, since Jesus died to present the Church blameless before himself.[2] Parachurches are good and needed ministries, but they are to be geared towards supporting the local church.

The content of the Great Commission

Matthew 28:19–20 says, "Therefore go and make disciples of all nations, baptizing them in the name of the Father and of the Son and of the Holy Spirit, and teaching them to obey everything I have commanded you." The command to make disciples entails telling people about Jesus, growing your church, and making converts; but it goes deeper than mere programs. Making disciples requires being a disciple of Jesus, because a disciple is a student and follower of Jesus.[3] To make disciples is to help new Christians grow into maturity in Christ, so that

---

[2] Colossians 1:18; 22; Ephesians 5:27.
[3] Luke 6:40.

they will follow him in all of life.[4] Such training involves equipping and modeling for them what Christian maturity is all about, so they can become Christian leaders.[5] Making disciples is intergenerational, so that the church stays healthy over the generations, faithful to the task of proclaiming biblical truth and the biblical gospel.[6]

Jesus commands his disciples to reach "all nations." While Jesus came first for Israel (as in, the Jewish people), he also came for the world—every tribe, tongue, nation, and people.[7] At the beginning of the early church, the disciples went to Jerusalem, but soon would go to the Gentiles of every nation—both peasants and kings.[8] Matthew's Gospel focuses on how the Kingdom of Christ belongs to everyone who hears it and who bears fruit for Jesus.[9]

The Early Church struggled to understand what Jesus meant by saying, "go to the nations." Even so, he said to "make disciples of the nations" and "you will be my witnesses in Jerusalem, and in all Judea and Samaria, and to the ends of the earth."[10] The apostles preached with the power of the Holy Spirit and did mighty works for the glory of God. The Lord raised men like Stephen, Philip, and Paul to bring the gospel to the Gentiles.[11]

Christians have been empowered with the message of glad tidings and good news, as Jesus preached in Luke 4:16-30. Such a message is liberating and is good news to captives. But

[4] Luke 9:23-27; 2 Peter 1:3-10.
[5] Ephesians 4:11-15.
[6] Titus 2:1-10.
[7] Revelation 7:9.
[8] Matthew 10:5, 18.
[9] Matthew 2:1-12; 4:15-16; 8:5-13; 13:38; 21:43; 24:14.
[10] Acts 1:8.
[11] Acts 7-9.

frequently, our hesitancy and fear have such a grip on our hearts; we need to go back and consider the Great Commission, to consider the source of this charge. *Every Christian* has been empowered by God to make disciples.[12]

Jesus' instruction

As with everything that Jesus says, the command to "make disciples" is provided with an explanation, telling Christians and local churches how to fulfill the task—that is, by traveling throughout the world, baptizing and teaching people. First, Christians are to "go into the world" to make disciples, not passively just allow the "world" (those without the Truth) to come to the Church. Christians are not pushy in reaching others, but we do have to be intentional in making disciples by taking the initiative. Christians do this by praying for the lost among our families, communities, and at our jobs/schools. Additionally, we are to share the gospel faithfully with the people we come into contact with. Every church should have a missionary heartbeat, both locally and internationally.

In the local church, Christians make disciples by preaching the gospel and then baptizing in the name of the Father and of the Son and the Holy Spirit those who confess Jesus as Lord.[13] When we baptize people at the local church, we are baptizing them in the name of Jesus, thus also confessing at such time that Jesus is equal with the God the Father and God the Holy Spirit. The sacrament of baptism asks Jesus' messengers to disciple people by calling them to identify with Jesus via public water immersion.

---

[12] Acts 1:6-8.
[13] Matthew 28:19.

Christians make disciples by "teaching them to obey everything I have commanded you."[14] Local churches must teach everything the Bible teaches, for in Scripture's sixty-six books we are taught everything we need for life and godliness.[15]

The Great Commission is so sweeping because of its fourfold use of the word *"all."* Jesus has *all authority* from God the Father. Disciples of Jesus are to make disciples by *teaching all* Jesus commands, fortifying themselves in and with the knowledge that he is with the people of God. Since Jesus loves the people of God, he closes, not with a command in the Great Commission, but with comfort. Jesus assured his disciples of his power and presence here at the close of his ministry that wherever they go, he will be with them.

Remember who is giving us these words in Matthew's Gospel. Matthew was once a despised tax collector and was not stronger than any of the other eleven disciples. Every disciple of Jesus can grow as Matthew did. The words and presence of the Lord Jesus transformed Matthew from a man of little faith to a man mightily used by God. Matthew grew by hearing the words of God, living in the presence of Jesus. Today, we can do the same by hearing the Word of God preached and by studying it. Jesus charges the people of God to grow into the fullness of discipleship, to live out our lives in his presence, and to fulfill the Great Commission.

Growing in discipleship to Jesus

To be a disciple is to be a student, and such studying requires that we live, not part of our lives, but our whole lives for Jesus. To be a growing and useful servant of Jesus, we need to say,

---

[14] Matthew 28:20.
[15] 2 Timothy 3:16–17; 2 Peter 1:20–21.

"Lord, here is my life, take and use it for your glory." What Jesus wants in discipleship is for all of our lives to be lived before him. The demands of discipleship are high—it will cost us everything.[16]

Many Christians are so distracted by life going on around them. There are only so many hours in a day, and there are so many things to do. But where in all of that is Jesus? Do you spend time with him throughout your day? Is Jesus in the midst of your marriage? Is Jesus amid your friendships? Is Jesus in the midst of your ministry? Or are you so distracted by all those good and necessary things that you are never concerned with whether Jesus is in any of those things?

As we learn about the Great Commission, what we are talking about is a whole life before the face of Jesus; because to be a disciple of Jesus is to be a student of Jesus.[17] Christians face distractions from every quarter and in every phase of life. There are good distractions in our lives and bad distractions. Good distractions can take our minds off of something negative and difficult in our lives. For example, I greatly enjoy watching football or golf, and/or reading about them. Since there's always something to read about both golf and football, I can occupy my time doing so, and it helps me get my mind off of whatever might be bothering me.

While such distractions can be helpful, they can also become a significant hindrance. For example, when I replace the priority of local church attendance with that of watching a major golf championship or an American football game, I've taken an enjoyable hobby into the realm of a *bad distraction*.

---

[16] Luke 14:25–33.
[17] Luke 6:40.

Since I can record anything I want on my DVR , there is really no need to prioritize it over anything else...ever (especially since there has never been a good reason to put watching TV first). But even if I didn't have a DVR, I need to prioritize God first and then my family.

The Great Commission is not *part of our lives* as Christians; Jesus doesn't call us to have *part of our lives* in submission to him. He calls for every area of life to be lived under the banner of his name and to be all-in for his glory. We may think the Great Commission is just making disciples of random people by talking to them, but disciple-making occurs over the kitchen counter or at the dinner table, while at the drive-through, and everywhere else we go. What we allow into our lives and our hearts affects the kind of disciple we are. And that's critical to understand, because the Great Commission is not a "great suggestion," but the *great command.*

Jesus calls for a radical type of discipleship that is centered and focused on him.[18] All of that means that we are to be all-in for Jesus, and our focus is to be wholly on loving him with our heads, hearts, and souls.[19] Good distractions can help us to unwind and relax, and there's nothing wrong with that. But even there, we can cross over the line so quickly from a "good thing" into the *ultimate* thing. The only ultimate thing in our lives must be Jesus and the work of his Great Commission.

Wrapping up section two

As we wrap up the second section of this book and head to the conclusion, I want to challenge you, dear reader. In the first section of this book, we considered how Jesus wants to stir our

---

[18] Luke 9:23–27.
[19] Matthew 22:37–40.

affections for himself to go beyond just knowing the "how" of what we do, to the "why" behind studying the Bible. It's in understanding the *why* that we get to the heart of the Christian faith.

In this section of this book, we've considered more of the "why" in regards to aspects of life in the church. See, it's not enough to know the right answers to these things apart from life transformation. It's precisely because you now know these things that you are to do them, practicing them in your everyday life. You do them because of the grace of God, through the Holy Spirit. In this, you are faithful to Jesus.

Jesus provides the grace to obey and the grace to follow him in all of life, both inside and outside the local church.[20] It takes the grace of God to sit through the preached Word, to deal with challenging people, and to interact with one another in love. But it's also important that we understand why we do all this—and that is to become more like Jesus. If our lives are so full that we have no time for each other, we are failing to be disciples. Jesus invites us to find rest in him and enjoy him.[21] It is good to be busy, but if we are more like Martha, who was so busy for Jesus that she missed out on sitting at his feet—unlike her sister, Mary—then we miss out on Jesus himself.[22]

You see, what we need is to sit at the feet of Jesus and learn. Every single one of us has full, busy lives. But, every so often, life distracts us from him. We are so busy with bad distractions, that we have no room in our lives for what should be the ultimate thing(s) of our lives, which are Christ, his Church, and making disciples of Jesus Christ.

---

[20] John 15:1–10.
[21] Matthew 11:28–30.
[22] Luke 10:38–42.

Your day will likely be very different from mine. My day is full of incoming emails, my phone buzzing, and messages popping up on social media with questions, prayer requests, or chats. And all of this is intermingled with editing articles, podcasts, author interviews, and other recordings. It is so easy to crowd out what is most important that I miss the point of it all—sharing the good news with people and ministering to his Church as I worship him. At the end of the day, Christians are to love the Lord and people.[23] It's because we are in the Word daily that we will earnestly desire to live our lives as committed disciples of Jesus in the local church.

As we wrap up section two, I merely want to challenge you to examine your life and to test to see if you love the Lord as much as you say you do, or if your love is only an expression of words. If you find that your actions are not living up to the words you speak, I want to encourage you to repent and turn to Jesus, who alone can lead you to repentance.[24] Even if all is "well and good" in our Christian walk, there is always room for growth in our lives.[25] And sometimes that growth is in realizing that, even with the good things, we can say no. Not every opportunity is meant for us, which is why we need to know and acknowledge our limits. We are finite creatures, and our God is infinite. Sometimes that "no" is an indication of spiritual maturity, just as much as the "yes," but either way, we need to be sitting at the feet of Jesus and learning from his heart through his Word; it is him alone who provides rest for the weary.[26]

---

[23] Matthew 22:37-40.
[24] 1 John 1:9.
[25] 1 Thessalonians 4:9-12.
[26] Matthew 11:28-30; 1 Corinthians 15:58.

Perhaps that's you today—weary and needing rest. Perhaps you are so busy with so many things that you never stop or pause to take in the beauty of life around you. I want to remind you that it is just as vital to the Great Commission that you learn to sit at the feet of Jesus. Disciples are not above their Master. Jesus does not need to sleep, since he is the God-Man, but he provides rest for our weary hearts and minds because he is our Sabbath rest.[27] Our ability to rest and relax reveals where our confidence is—in the Lord, or in ourselves. Our ability to sleep well (or not sleep well) reveals where our trust and confidence is with regards to the sovereignty of God.[28] Are we plagued with worry and anxiety, or are we trusting God in all things?

The Great Commission is not "the great suggestion." It is a *command* for a reason; a command to be engaged and to live before the face of God. So, wherever you are in your walk with God today, I challenge you to consider and count the cost of being a disciple of Jesus. The Great Commission is meant to be lived in the local church, which then disperses to the rest of the world. The Great Commission is a lifestyle, grounded in Christ and empowered by the Holy Spirit. The Holy Spirit provides opportunities for encouragement, evangelism, and discipleship. In all of it, the Holy Spirit aims to make much of Jesus and enables the disciples of Christ to grow in him. It is from his work in their lives that they can carry forth glad tidings of good news for the glory of God. As you flip the page to the final chapter of this book, we will conclude this book considering faithfulness in every area of life.

---

[27] Matthew 11:28–30; Hebrews 4:9–10.
[28] Psalm 4:8.

CONCLUSION:
FAITHFULNESS TO THE LORD
IN EVERY SPHERE OF LIFE

For the Christian, the goal of our life is to become like Jesus[1] and then to be with him forever. Faithfulness to God is a perennial issue because it demonstrates whether we are living rightly, according to the Word of God, or whether we are living for ourselves. The options the Bible presents the Christian are *faithfulness to God* or *disobedience to God*.[2] The first obedience is made possible by union with Christ, who is and always will be faithful, while the latter is possible because we are walking in our own power instead of in the daily strength the Lord provides by his grace.

God's faithfulness to his people means that he will always act in accordance with his revealed character in his Word, which is true for the past, present, and future. 1 Kings 8:56 says, "Not one word has failed of all the good promises he gave." The Lord God is eternally reliable, steadfast, and unwavering because faithfulness is one of his attributes. With that said, it's essential to explain that the Lord doesn't have to work at being faithful like we do. He is faithful at the core of his being. Put another way, faithfulness is a vital part of who the Lord is.[3] In the faithfulness of his revealed character, he protects the

---

[1] Romans 8:28-30.
[2] Luke 6:43; John 14:21; 23.
[3] Psalm 89:8; Hebrews 13:8.

91

people of God from evil,[4] sets limits on our temptation,[5] forgives all sin,[6] and sanctifies us.[7]

Becoming like Jesus means growing in our life-long pursuit of faithfulness. The Word of God is littered with the consequences of unfaithfulness. Such warnings are given because, as the old hymn "Come Thou Fount of Every Blessing" says, we are "prone to wander...prone to leave the God I love."[8] Often, if we're honest with God and ourselves, our hearts are fickle, even despite our best motivations to honor him.[9]

To combat our tendencies towards unfaithfulness, we need to consider how faithfulness affects every relationship we have in our lives. We do this when we are sharpened by the Word and equipped by the Holy Spirit. Scripture teaches that "the just will live by faith."[10] The Lord God is faithful to his people, and by grace, as we grow in our faithfulness to him through devoting ourselves to the Word, to prayer, and to living life in the local church, we will hear, "Well done, good and faithful servant!"[11]

Faithfulness to the Lord entails all of what we've considered in this book so far. Such a life honors the Lord and brings him maximum joy and glory. Bringing the Lord maximum joy and honor, by living rightly before him, is the concern of every Christian because it is a demonstration of our *obedience*. This obedience is not only evidence of our faith, but the source of our maximum joy. But our obedience is not for ourselves alone.

---

[4] 2 Thessalonians 3:3.
[5] 1 Corinthians 10:13.
[6] 1 John 1:9.
[7] 1 Corinthians 1:9; Philippians 1:6.
[8] Robert Robinson, "Come thou fount of every blessing," stanza 4.
[9] Proverbs 20:6; Jeremiah 17:9; Matthew 26:75.
[10] Habakkuk 2:4.
[11] Matthew 25:23.

It also demonstrates to a watching world that we don't just "say the right words," we live by them, and are aiming to live rightly before the Lord. As we become faithful, Word-shaped people of God, devoted to prayer and involved in the local church, God will use us to extinguish the wave of biblical illiteracy permeating our culture in our days. Such obedient and righteous lives are what I am aiming to encourage readers toward in writing this book. It is my hope that your hearts, minds, and affections will be set on the glory of God, so you will become (even more) men and women of character that God desires you to be—both in our personal lives, and in our lives before the watching world. The Holy Spirit takes the Word and plants it deep into your heart and life, thus bringing honor to the Son Jesus, who paid the ultimate penalty so that you might be forgiven. Therefore, walk in newness of life and live a life worthy of the calling you've received from him.[12]

---

[12] Colossians 1:10; Ephesians 4:1.

ACKNOWLEDGEMENTS

To my Lord and Savior Jesus: Thank you for saving me from my sins with your costly blood and for rising again from the dead so that I might have new life in You. Thank you, Lord, for always loving me and disciplining me as Your son when I need it. Thank you, Lord, for always being with me, and for holding me fast by sovereign grace. I love you, Lord, and pray you will be pleased to use this book to help the people of God grow in your Word and the grace you alone provide to them in Christ.

To my beautiful wife and best friend Sarah, thank you for always loving me with the love of Christ, encouraging me on good and bad days with the grace of God, and for your help as I worked through writing this book and then editing it. Thank you for not only being a godly woman but helping me to grow to be a man of God. Thank you for all your help in becoming a better editor, writer, and follower of Jesus over the past thirteen and a half years of our marriage. I love you, value you, and treasure you beyond words, my love.

To my parents, Jim and Betty Jenkins, I'm so thankful for both of you for your prayers, love, encouragement, and for always making sure I was in churches that loved the Word of God and the grace of our Lord Jesus when I was growing up.

To Mike Beaudin, thank you for your continued encouragement and friendship. It's no small thing to say, but without the Lord using you in my life, I wouldn't be anywhere near where I am now in the grace of God. Thank you for lovingly investing in me and continuing to do so; I'm thankful to our Lord for you.

To the many people over the years who have encouraged me to keep on writing through many challenges in my life, and who walked with me through those challenges, I offer my heartfelt thank you to the Lord for you.

SCRIPTURE INDEX

CPSIA information can be obtained
at www.ICGtesting.com
Printed in the USA
BVHW040211150321
602540BV00019B/848

9 781989 174869